Advance Praise for *Capturing Customers.com!*

*"I have known George Colombo for over a decade and if there is one thing I can say, George "gets it." With all the hype surrounding the Internet, he cuts through and gets to what really is valuable and what really works. George and I both have preached for years that technology for technology's sake is worthless. Useful, practical technology applied to real world problems is what really pays off. Thousands of companies have wasted millions of dollars on projects that haven't delivered. In "***Capturing Customers.com***," George does a great job of helping readers understand how to apply practical technology to practical problems that will impact a company's top and bottom lines. I heartily endorse George's intelligent and balanced approach to applying what is truly great about the Internet to everyday selling and marketing problems. It can pay off for readers in big and profitable ways."*

—Pat Sullivan
CEO, Interact Commerce Corporation

"I have been viciously critical of 90 percent of all make-money-via-Internet material. In too many ways, "dotcom" has become synonymous with "B.S." George Colombo's book is different. For one thing, it deals intelligently with bigger issues, such as responding to the current shift in power between buyers and sellers. For another, it correctly puts the Internet in context as media that must fit a complete marketing plan, not some magical replacement for all other tools. Here is sound thinking in a world gone e-mad!"

—Dan S. Kennedy
Author, *No Rules* and *The Ultimate Marketing Plan*,
Editor, *No B.S. Marketing Letter*

"George Colombo has always been a pioneer when it comes to teaching sales and marketing people how to use technology effectively. His new book, **Capturing Customers.com***, finds him once again on the cutting edge. If you've been skeptical about all the hype surrounding the Internet, George Colombo's highly readable book is just what you've been waiting for."*

—Dr. Tony Alessandra
Author, *Collaborative Selling* and *Charisma*

Advance Praise for *Capturing Customers.com*!

"In a field dominated by self-appointed visionary strategists, George Colombo—himself a master salesman—puts the "e" of "e-business" in context. He's written an invaluable guide for businesspeople who understand that their proper e-strategy is to profit from the Internet, not simply to be there. Or as George himself says, "Being on the Internet, in and of itself, does not constitute a business objective." If you're looking for useless, feel-good punditry, look elsewhere. If you're looking for dozens of ideas you can use tomorrow, read **Capturing Customers.com.***"*

—Bob Lewis
Author, *Lewis's Laws,*
Co-author, *Selling on the Net,*
Columnist, *InfoWorld*

"Stunningly insightful, a must read book for anyone trying to capture a customer in the Internet-gone-mad era. George combines his business wisdom and the facts to show how to maneuver through the mine fields of clicks, bricks, and tricks."

—Cheryl Currid
Author, *Computing Strategies for Reengineering Your Organization* and 13 other business and technology books, President, Currid & Company, a high-tech research firm

Capturing Customers.com

Radical Strategies for Selling and Marketing in a Wired World

By George Colombo

CAREER
PRESS
Franklin Lakes, NJ

**Not connected or affiliated with Patricia Seybold
or The Patricia Seybold Group, Inc.**

CAPTURING CUSTOMERS.COM
Edited by Jodi Brandon
Typesetting by John J. O'Sullivan
Cover design by Lu Rossman
Printed in the U.S.A. by Book-mart Press

To order this title, please call toll-free 1-800-CAREER-1 (NJ and Canada:
201-848-0310) to order using VISA or MasterCard, or for further
information on books from Career Press.

CAREER
PRESS

The Career Press, Inc., 3 Tice Road, PO Box 687,
Franklin Lakes, NJ 07417
www.careerpress.com

Library of Congress Cataloging-in-Publication Data

Colombo, George.
   Capturing customers.com : radical strategies for selling and market
ing in a wired world / by George Colombo.
      p. cm.
   Includes index.
   ISBN 1-56414-507-7 (cloth)
      1. Internet marketing--Handbooks, manuals, etc. I. Title

HF5415.1265 .C64 2001
658.8'4--dc21   00-065103

Dedication

This book is dedicated to Anthony and Joseph. You guys make me proud to be your dad every single day.

Acknowledgments

You've heard it before so I won't belabor the point, but the truth is that even as modest a book as the one you're holding in your hands cannot come together without the help and support of a number of people. In my case, I was truly fortunate to have a terrific group of friends and colleagues who were invaluable—in all kinds of different ways—in making this book possible.

Laura Collins ably handled all of the administrative stuff and kept the office humming while I closeted myself away to do the research for this book and hammer out the pages. I appreciate her keeping secret the fact that the office runs far better when I'm not there.

My agent, Jeff Herman, kept plugging away with the proposal for this book when others would have quit. That's why there are lots of agents but just one Jeff Herman.

Ron Fry and Anne Brooks had the good sense to publish this book and to hang in there when the bad guys in Boston tried to throw a wrench in the machinery.

I've worked with Ginger Conlon for a while now and she is truly an editor extraordinaire. All of the interview segments in this book are as good as they are (and they are very good) because of her deft touch.

Ginger Cooper, Cheryl Currid, and Mark Eggleston were all extremely helpful and supportive when I needed it. If you ever need a sanity check, a different perspective, a sympathetic ear while you vent (a regular undertaking for me), or guidance when you're in need of information, you could not do better than to have this group at your disposal.

Jim Jeter has been helping me keep my head screwed on straight (er, sort of) for longer than either of us would care to admit.

No one has a more keenly developed BS meter than Dan Kennedy. And no one "gets" marketing any better than he does. If I can ever learn as much as he's probably forgotten, I'll be in good shape.

If it wasn't for David Korzenik, this book would have some kind of lame title that I'd have hated every time I saw it. If you ever get a nasty lawyer letter someday, you'd want to have David on your speed dial.

Bob Lewis is a very, very smart guy who (1) is also very, very funny and (2) lets me call him to pick his brain whenever I want. You can't get any better than that.

Seth Godin, Christopher Lochhead, Don Peppers, Chris Pirillo, David Weinberger, and Barton Weitz were all generous with their time and gracious enough to allow this book to benefit from their insights. The fact that people as brilliant as this group would make the time for me to interview them for this book is exactly what I was talking about when I said that I was fortunate. (Often, it's better to be lucky than to be good.)

And, of course, my wife, Sandy. There isn't a single positive thing that I've done over the past 17 years that she didn't make possible. I can't imagine any of it without her. (The screw-ups, on the other hand, were all mine.)

Contents

Introduction

I know what you're thinking, and you're right: You deserve an answer to the question, "Why should I read another book about e-business?" After all, it probably seems as though everything that could possibly be said about doing business on the Web has already been said. In fact, it not only seems as though it's all been said, but it's been beaten to death over and over again by an apparently endless parade of self-appointed gurus and consultants who were doing who-knows-what before they hopped on to the Internet bandwagon. So, what makes this book different?

For starters, this is emphatically *not* another book about how to "dotcom." In case you hadn't noticed, things are not going too well lately in the world of dotcoms. The stream of dotcom failures began with a trickle, but it didn't take very long for it to turn into a full-scale flood! (It wouldn't be useful to try to chronicle all of the dotcom disappointments here, because any list would be hopelessly out of date before the ink on the pages was dry. If you're interested, though, there's an entertaining Web site that's devoted solely to tracking the failures of yesterday's Web wonders. The site is designed as a parody of *Fast Company*, a magazine that covers the world of business on the Internet. Appropriately enough, it's called *www.fuckedcompany.com.*)

Looking back on it, the whole premise behind the dotcom hysteria was more than a little shaky. We were supposed to believe that old-style businesses were becoming obsolete right before our eyes, that they couldn't compete with these nimble new startups that weren't weighed down by stores, sales offices, or salespeople. We were told by one Web guru after another that customers were ready to abandon their old buying behaviors in favor of the convenience, interactivity, and immediacy of the Web. The ever-growing list of dotcom failures is pretty clear evidence that things didn't work out quite as planned.

The Trouble With Dotcoms

When you think about it, there were a couple of fairly obvious chinks in the armor. The biggest one of these underscores one of the basic premises of this book: All other things being equal, it's better to have a physical presence in your marketplace than to not have one. I won't go into too much detail right here because I'm going to discuss this principle in much greater detail in Chapter Two. For right now, though, let's just say that credibility is always in issue when it comes to buying decisions (this is true for both business customers and consumers) and that it's tough to be credible when you're virtual.

Another flaw in the strategy of most dotcom companies is that they were counting on some pretty dramatic changes in the buying behaviors of their prospective customers. It didn't take them too long to find out that it's easy to go broke waiting for customers to make radical and fundamental changes in their buying behaviors. It's not that such changes can't happen. It's that they take time. In the business and technology worlds, the penalty for being too early is often greater than the penalty for being too late. You can congratulate yourself for having foresight, but it's not much consolation when you've run out of money and out of time.

Now that the dust is settling and the initial wave of Internet enthusiasm has run its course, it's time to take a fresh, dispassionate look at how technology is changing the business of attracting, acquiring, and nurturing customers. That is my mission for this book. Yes, the promises of the Web consultants and the first dotcom companies were overblown. But the truth is that, even if it happens more slowly than we were told it would, technology is going to cause profound changes in how business is conducted. In particular, it's going to dramatically change the nature of your relationships with your customers.

What you're going to find in the pages of this book is a guide that's designed to help you navigate through the maze of issues that surround this whole business of using technology to enhance your sales and marketing efforts. It's going to help you match your technology initiatives with the wants and needs of your customers. It will help you understand the dynamics of a changing marketplace so that you're not too far out on the cutting edge. At the same time, it will give you essential insights into the possibilities that the Internet and its related technologies offer so that you don't run the risk of missing any significant opportunities.

Throughout this entire book, you're going to be exposed to some very specific strategies and techniques that you'll be able to apply to your business. Of course, depending on your business and your marketplace, not every example or idea is going to perfectly fit your specific needs. Don't try to shoehorn in a technique that doesn't feel right. There'll be some ideas that you'll choose to rework for your particular situation. And there will certainly be some that you'll find interesting but will ultimately decide are not for you. (That's fine, too.)

One of the biggest problems with a lot of what's been promoted by the first generation of Web gurus is a kind of one-size-fits-all approach. The truth is that Internet business is no different from conventional business in the sense that there are lots of business models and approaches that can work, depending on your market and your product. Nordstrom functions pretty well, but so does Wal-Mart. They're both retail stores, but they aren't interchangeable. You couldn't sell Nordstrom products Wal-Mart-style or vice versa. You need congruence among your product (or service), your customer, and your selling and marketing approach. That principle doesn't change just because you've added the Internet to the equation.

The Biggest Lie of All

One of the most damaging and misleading statements about the Internet is something that's been repeated so many times, by so many "experts" that I've lost count. Here it is: The Internet changes everything. I understand that a statement like this is supposed to be a harmless bit of hyperbole, designed to get people thinking and to understand that something important is going on. Unfortunately, when it gets repeated over and over again, people tend to start taking it literally and the results are disastrous.

Here's what I say: The Internet changes a lot of things, but it doesn't change *everything*. For example, the Internet doesn't change your customer's underlying needs. Your customers approach every transaction with a unique and specific set of needs and wants. Those needs and wants don't change just because a transaction becomes technology-enabled. And your deployment of Internet technology—no matter how

skillfully it's done—will never take precedence over th
needs and wants. If marketing and selling your products a.
services is your objective (and if it isn't, then this book is definitely *not* for you!), then Internet technology only makes sense
when it can be deployed in a way that addresses your customers' needs and wants.

Another thing the Internet doesn't change is the ultimate
need to be profitable, or to at least see a way to get there without relying on a torturous set of assumptions that call for unlikely changes in the behavior of your marketplace. "Eyeballs"
is not an objective by itself. It is a means to an end and that end
is a profitable business model. The oldest cliché in the world is
that, when you're losing money on every customer, you can't
make it up in volume!

I want to make one last point about how the Internet is
likely to impact your business (and here is another basic
premise of this book): Old models and media seldom vanish.
Instead, they usually redefine themselves for a different kind
of usefulness. As management guru Peter Drucker recently put
it in *Forbes,* "New channels of distribution are typically addi-
tions and complements rather than replacements. Television,
for example, did not kill radio or magazines or books. The new
medium, TV, walked off with much of the growth but the other
media continued to thrive and grow, too." Keep that in mind
the next time you hear someone tell you how the Internet is
going to destroy retail stores, field-based salespeople, or some
other mode of selling or marketing.

What I hope will be clear by the time you get to the end of
this book is that a much more likely scenario is that the Internet will complement, augment, and enhance the ways in which
you're already relating to your customers. Sure, there will be
instances of pure dotcom operations that are successful. Remember what I said earlier about how the market supports a
variety of approaches. (For a variety of reasons, for example, I

believe that *Amazon.com* will be one of the dotcom winners, and I'll explain why later in this book.) But for most businesses, the Internet needs to be looked at as one more tool in your sales and marketing toolbox.

The Internet Cannot Do It All

The key to making it work is to discover the right match between your business tools and your business objectives. There will be some tasks for which the Internet is absolutely the perfect tool. In fact, you're going to identify certain things that you'll be able to do with Internet technology that would simply be impossible to accomplish with any of the other tools at your disposal. But for all of the Internet's power, there will be some things that are best accomplished with a fax, a phone call, or a face-to-face meeting. You wouldn't try to drive a nail with a saw. A saw might be a great tool, but when it comes to driving nails, a hammer is still your best bet. The Internet is a great tool, too, but it's not the best tool for everything.

When you're done with this book, you'll have a much better handle on exactly how to use this terrific tool to help you identify, attract, cultivate, and capture customers in today's wired world. And you'll have a better understanding of how it can be integrated into your overall sales and marketing toolbox with the rest of the tools at your disposal. After all, as you'll see very clearly in Chapters One and Five, the ultimate objective of *all* of your sales and marketing efforts should be *capturing customers*.

Some Additional Perspectives

But you don't have to take my word for all of this! In the course of putting this book together, I reviewed the work of some of the most insightful and original thinkers around when it comes to the kinds of new sales and marketing approaches that will be successful in the years to come. Rather than try to distill their thinking into some sort of *Reader's Digest* condensation, I sought these people out and spoke with them directly about some of the ideas that you're going to read about in this book. You'll find these conversations scattered throughout the book.

You're going to find some points about which these experts disagree. That's certainly to be expected when you're talking about a group of people as intellectually independent as this one is. After all, the people I spoke with are all brilliant, intensely original thinkers. On the other hand, I think you'll find a certain consensus among them about the broad strokes of where the worlds of sales and marketing are heading as the Internet weaves itself into the fabric of our everyday commercial activities.

In any event, there's no need to gild the lily. I'll let these conversations speak for themselves.

Moving Beyond the Limitations of "Web Centricity"

Chapter 1

A Survey of the Battlefield

It's impossible to fight a war successfully if you're not intimately familiar with the terrain. Even superior resources can't help you much if you don't have a good idea of the environment in which you're fighting. Without a reliable survey of the battlefield, every move you make is potentially dangerous; there are unexpected problems waiting for you around every corner. Most important, though, is the fact that it's almost impossible to know if the steps you're taking are moving you closer to your objective or farther away.

The battle for the hearts, mind, and dollars of your customers operates along the same lines. You've got to know the territory if you're going to win. That's what this chapter is all about. I want to provide you with as clear a picture as possible of the business environment where you'll be competing. It's critically important that you understand the basic characteristics of today's hyper-competitive, wired business environment if you're going to have any chance at all of putting a winning plan together.

If fact, the adjectives I just used to describe today's business environment (hyper-competitive and wired) represent the two characteristics that are going to be most important as you design, implement, and refine your sales and marketing plans.

The Shifting Balance of Power in the Marketplace

Let's begin with a look at what I call the hyper-competitive nature of the marketplace. If you're going to be successful, you need to start by embracing this fundamental principle: The balance of power in the marketplace has shifted dramatically and irrevocably from you (the seller) to your customer (the buyer). This is more than a change in the tide. It's a gigantic tidal wave, crashing over the entire marketplace. It's as equally true for so-called business-to-business sales as it is for consumer sales. You can try to resist it, but you're likely to have about as much success as you'd have if you stepped off the roof of a 10-story building and tried to resist gravity. As with gravity, it's going to be there whether you like it or not. And, as with gravity, you're going to have a lot more success aligning your efforts to take advantage of it than you will by ignoring it or trying to move in the opposite direction.

This shift in the balance of power began some time ago (most analysts will tell you that it started in the early 1970s), but it accelerated rapidly with the dawn of the age of the Internet. Basically, there are two factors that have caused the shift: options and information. At least one of these factors is at work in literally every market you can think of, and most markets are feeling the results of both.

Balance of Power Factor #1: Buyers Have More Options Than Ever Before.

When I was a kid, my father bought a Volvo. By today's standard, that doesn't seem like such an extraordinary thing, but at the time, it was pretty outrageous. At that time the automobile market was dominated by four companies. General Motors was the clear and unquestioned market leader. Just one of GM's divisions at the time, Chevrolet, was selling almost as many cars as everyone else put together! Ford came next, followed by Chrysler. A now-defunct company called American Motors brought up the rear. In those days, any kind of foreign car was looked upon as exotic. In fact, the original Volkswagen Beetle was still such a novelty that Beetle owners would wave at each other if they passed on the road. A car from Sweden was so out of the ordinary that it was almost incomprehensible.

What could it possibly have been like to be an American automaker in that kind of environment? It probably isn't much of an exaggeration to say that you could almost grab a profitable share of the market just by showing up. The marketplace was eager to buy what you had to sell, and you had a finite number of competitors to sell against. I'd bet that there are more than a few General Motors executives who remember those days wistfully!

Today's competitive environment for automakers is obviously quite different. Foreign competition is no longer exotic. It's commonplace and it not only includes mainstream competitors from Germany and Sweden, but also ones from Japan, Great Britain, and Korea. Obviously, the dynamic of competition is a lot tougher with so many competitive players. Post-World War II recovery and the globalization of the marketplace helped to spawn new competitors in the automobile industry, but other industries are dealing with the same result, albeit for different reasons.

Consider the television industry, for example. I was recently visiting at a friend's house and he showed me an old newspaper that he had saved. It was an issue of *The New York Post* from 1963. We took the paper out of its protective wrapper and were thumbing through it, looking at the news items and the ads, when we came to the page that featured television listings. The entire television schedule for the largest market in the country, including brief program descriptions, fit on less than two thirds of a single page. I'm not talking about just the prime time listings, either; I'm talking about 24 hours of programming!

The difference between the number of options available then and today is obviously several orders of magnitude. I have no doubt that test patterns in 1963 probably garnered the kind of market share that cable channels today have to fight for.

In industry after industry, marketers are seeing the same proliferation of competitors. In some industries, it's the result of globalization and lowered trade barriers. In other industries, it's the result of technological advances that have lowered barriers to entry. Still other industries have gotten there as a result of deregulation. From a sales and marketing standpoint, the cause is less important than the result. The bottom line is that it's a great deal more difficult to deal with a marketplace that has more players against whom you've got to compete.

Balance of Power Factor #2: Buyers Have More Information Than Ever Before.

Consider the situation of a typical life insurance salesperson 10 or 15 years ago. He'd march into a prospect's home and, if he did a good job with presentation, he had a good chance of walking out with a signed policy and a check. The sale was usually made on the basis of one type of emotional appeal or another, and it was a rare prospect, indeed, who even thought about soliciting competitive bids on a similar policy.

In fact, even if a prospect was interested in doing so, there was no convenient place to go to get the information. The best alternative available for most prospects would have been to contact another agent and sit through another presentation in order to get a single additional quote. It hardly seemed worth it. When it came to balance of power based on the amount and quality of information available, the seller was clearly in the driver's seat.

Today, that same prospect has a world of information at his or her fingertips. Web sites such as *Selectquote.com* can scan the offerings of dozens of insurance companies in just a few minutes, allowing the prospect to quickly and easily find the cheapest policy possible. The insurance industry isn't the only one that has to contend with the widespread availability of price information. Similar sites exist for almost any other industry or marketplace you can think of.

And it's not just pricing information that's readily available. In the retail computer industry, for example, *Cnet.com* provides product specifications and qualitative feedback on a variety of products, including computers, printers, cameras, scanners, music players, and monitors. Today's buyer is no longer dependent on the sometimes-questionable information provided by the salesperson in a computer store. Instead, he or she often comes into the store armed with more information than the salesperson has.

If you consider these two factors (options and information), it doesn't take long to see why the balance of power between sellers and buyers has shifted dramatically. Sellers once approached sales situations with the commercial equivalent of a bow and arrow. Buyers came relatively "unarmed," and the results were predictable. Today, sellers still have their bows and arrows. The difference is that today's buyer is now armed with modern warfare. Sellers can't win with the same old strategies, weapons, and tactics.

What Doesn't Work

So, if you're a seller, what's the answer? There are a few things that we know will *not* work. One of those is trying to compete on price alone. Obviously, when your customer has access to vast amounts of competitive pricing information, you're usually limited to playing within certain general pricing parameters. Most businesses cannot sustain pricing levels that are significantly outside the boundaries set by the marketplace. (This is not true in every case, however. It is often possible to stake out a "super premium" position in the market. One company I know of, for example, has staked out a profitable niche in the golf industry by selling a set of clubs for more than $5,000!)

The lowest price in the marketplace, though, is not a good place for most businesses to be. The most obvious flaw to this approach is that there is always going to be someone who is willing to go just a little lower. This is usually a competitor who has little else to offer. As a result, if you try to position yourself in the marketplace based on price alone, you're constantly at the whim of your least capable competitors. Clearly, that's a poor competitive position.

A bigger problem with positioning yourself based on price alone is that such an approach forces you to marry with a business model that provides you with few resources to devote to the long-term care of your customers. In today's hyper-competitive business environment, a business model that does not focus on customer satisfaction is likely to be fatally flawed in the long run.

Another approach that's almost impossible to sustain is trying to secure a place in the market based on the uniqueness of your product or service. In today's business environment, if you come up with a winner, you can count on a competitor entering the marketplace with a similar offering in a breathtakingly brief period of time. In fact, with the exception of the pharmaceutical industry, which operates under the umbrella of protective regulation, the time it takes for your competitors to copy your winners is getting shorter and shorter. This trend has been described by marketing guru Dan Kennedy, who's an expert in the infomercial industry. In that industry, he estimates that if a new exercise product proves successful, for example, it's likely to get knocked off in less than 90 days. That's not 90 days before the copycat product is conceived; it's 90 days before the product is designed, the commercial is shot, and the whole thing is on the air!

Competitors in different industries will react more or less quickly than that. The important point here is that you can't count on the uniqueness of your product or service to convey a competitive advantage in the marketplace over a sustained period of time. If you're successful, count on your competitors finding a way to cruise in your slipstream.

There's Really Only One Answer

The only sustainable advantage that you can create in the marketplace is a superior relationship with your customers, based on your ability to deliver a better-quality customer experience. In one sense, let's face it, this is not exactly news. After all, prior to the advent of the Internet, companies such as Nordstrom and L.L. Bean built legendary businesses based on this principle. The *real* news here is the fact that not only is this principle more important than ever before in a less forgiving selling and marketing environment, but also that the Internet provides businesses with tremendously expanded opportunities to implement it effectively. This is great news for you, because only the smartest, most disciplined marketers will do the thinking that's necessary to take advantage of the opportunities at hand. The fact that you're reading this book gives you a meaningful head start in your market.

Of course, the specific steps required to deliver a better quality experience to your customers over time—and to capitalize on that experience from a sales and marketing standpoint—will vary from one business to another. Still, there's a basic procedure that's going to apply no matter what your product or service is or who you're selling to.

Step #1:
Make contact.

Naturally, the first step in any selling and marketing process is to get in contact with people who are likely to buy whatever it is that you're selling. A great deal of the Web's initial appeal to businesspeople was an implicit promise: If you were on the Web, customers from all over the world were going to track you down. As you'll see in Chapter 3, that promise didn't quite pan out. In fact, for many businesses, the cost of acquiring a customer on the Web turned out to be several times higher than the cost of acquiring that same customer through more traditional means. (As you'll see in Chapter 3, though, there are some effective methods that you'll learn for acquiring customers on the Web inexpensively.)

Step #2:
Develop the ability to sustain contact.

On or off the Web, it is astonishing how much time, effort, and money businesses put in to the quest for customers, only to let potential prospects slip through their fingers if a sale isn't made immediately. It's unbelievable! Imagine this scenario: You're at a party and are introduced to someone who is not only bright and witty but is also extremely attractive. You spend a half hour or so getting to know each other and you both seem to be enjoying the process. Then, for one reason or another, your new friend has to run off suddenly. Wouldn't it make sense to ask for a phone number? Of course it would.

The same principle applies to the "courtship" of a prospective customer. You can deliver a sensational marketing message but your prospect might not be ready to buy, for any number of reasons. Maybe he or she just bought a similar product or service and isn't ready to buy again. Maybe your prospect's daughter is getting married next week and he or she just can't concentrate on your offer right now. The reason could be anything. It really doesn't matter. What matters is that you've already made a big investment in finding this individual. Why not make a small investment in staying in touch so that you're at the forefront of your prospect's consciousness when he or she is finally ready to buy?

Step #3:
Deliver value.

If you do a good job with Step #2, sooner or later you're going to have an opportunity to close the deal and make a sale. This is a real moment of truth. You've got to deliver value here, or it's going to be very difficult to continue with the rest of the process.

The good news, though, is that Internet technology provides tremendous opportunities to enhance the value that you deliver to your customers without significantly increasing your costs. (This is true, by the way, whether your make the sale on the Web or not.)

Step #4:
Cultivate the relationship.

On or off the Internet, here's the step in the process where most businesses drop the ball. You cannot win in today's business environment by accumulating a succession of one-time transactions. This is true *no matter how many of them you're able to put together.*

We'll explore this principle in much more depth in Chapter 5. For the time being, the thing you need to remember is that it's essential to be proactive in maintaining your relationship with customers beginning immediately after the initial transaction. A useful rule of thumb is that after the initial sale, the value of your customer diminishes by 5 percent every month that goes by without some kind of contact from you.

In today's business environment—no matter what business you're in—your customer list is your most valuable asset, much more valuable than your capital equipment or inventory. And yet most businesses are content to let the value of that asset diminish steadily.

Historically, one reason for this apparent willingness to abandon customers after an initial transaction was the fact that the cost of staying in touch was not justified by the value of any expected future transactions. As you'll learn in Chapters 7 and 8, the "frictionless" quality of Internet-based communication changes that equation radically.

Step #5:
Escalate the terms of engagement.

Now it's time for the big payoff. Most of your customers will be content to transact business with you at a "normal" level. Depending on your product or service, you may find that, over time, you'll be able to increase the responsiveness of a select group of customers. And, ultimately, you may be able to cultivate a subset of that group to the point of becoming "hyper-responsive."

For example, one consultant I know periodically sells audiotape-based information products, typically priced between $300 and $500 each, to his customer base of business clients. Approximately 3 percent of his clients have reached this "hyper-responsive" level. What does that mean? In this particular case, these clients have instructed him to keep their credit cards on file and to automatically ship them anything he publishes. You don't need me to tell you that this type of client is inordinately profitable.

Step #5 is where you deliberately and systematically orchestrate a progressively more trusting and committed relationship with your customer. In Step #2, I used the analogy of a courtship. To carry that analogy a step further, think of Step #5 as moving the relationship from dating through engagement all the way to marriage. The important point is that, at the end of the process, the relationship between you and your customer is as solid as possible—and that it got that way because of your deliberate guidance.

The Impact of Technology

At the beginning of this chapter, I mentioned that there were two characteristics of today's business environment that you ought to be considering in every aspect of your sales and marketing planning. We spent a considerable amount of time discussing one of these (the hyper-competitive nature of the marketplace). Let's take a moment to consider the other characteristic: the fact that the business environment is "wired." In other words, we're all now connected to this giant network called the Internet.

There are a couple of elements that represent the subtext of everything else you're going to read in this book. The first is that the cost structure of many of your sales and marketing activities can change drastically if you deploy technology effectively. For example, I talked about making regular contact with your existing customers. This is not a new idea, of course. In fact, a guy named Joe Girard, probably the greatest retail car salesman that industry ever produced, was legendary for the monthly notes and cards he sent to his clients. If you were selling a $25,000 product, the economics of contacting a customer 36 times over the course of a three-year average sale cycle always made sense, even if you were writing each note by hand or using a typewriter. (Not that everyone in that business actually *did* that; it's just that it always made sense!)

Before the Internet, the economic justification for regular customer contact became less and less clear as the value of each individual transaction decreased. Sure, it made sense for a $25,000 car, but what about a $1,000 refrigerator? How about a $300 vacuum cleaner? What about a $75 putter?

The whole economic picture changes, though, with the introduction of technology. The cost of each piece of customer communication over the Internet is, effectively, zero. Sales and marketing efforts that were not feasible before make perfect sense now.

The other aspect of technology's impact that you'll want to consider is more elusive but, potentially, much more valuable. Every day, technology is creating ways to do things that were simply not possible before. You'll hear more about this, in much greater detail, in Chapter 4, but here's the thing to remember right now: As a business owner or senior sales/marketing executive, you might not think of yourself as a technology "geek," but you can create a considerable advantage for your company in the marketplace if you keep an eye on what's going on in the world of technology—particularly what's happening on the Internet. Get in the habit of thinking inductively.

As a businessperson, you're probably used to deductive reasoning. In other words, you arrive at a solution after examining the various elements of a problem. Deductive reasoning, in this context, is exactly the opposite approach. It means starting with a "solution" (in this case, a new technological innovation) and then reviewing your sales and marketing practices to see if there's some place that it can be used effectively.

The fact that today's marketplace is hyper-competitive and wired signifies that several important changes are taking place. In the next chapter, though, you're going to see a few aspects of the marketplace that aren't likely to change any time soon.

Stores and Salespeople Aren't Going Away

The battle between the Internet and more traditional means of doing business, such as salespeople, sales offices, and retail stores (disdainfully referred to by Web cognoscenti as "bricks and mortar"), was supposed to be a slam dunk. There was no way that conventional sales and marketing channels were going to be able to compete with the nimbleness of doing business on the Web. All sorts of Web experts (most of whom were undeterred by the fact that they didn't have any actual experience in conventional sales or marketing management roles) were eager to explain how the contest was going to be a rout. Actually, it turned into a rout in much the same way that Mike Tyson's fight with Buster Douglas turned into a rout.

Barely a week goes by without another dotcom enterprise somehow going bust. In fact, the phenomenon is so pervasive that *Fortune* magazine has launched a regular sidebar feature called "Dot Com Deathwatch" that chronicles the demise of former Web stars, such as *Toysmart.com* and *Boo.com,* that have either filed for bankruptcy or closed up shop altogether.

George Colony, CEO of Massachusetts-based Forrester Research, one of the rare consulting firms that managed even a moderate amount of skepticism in the midst of mind-boggling amounts of hype, published a scathing denunciation of dotcom companies and their managers. George pointed out that the business thinking of those managers is "centered on simplistic and clichéd mental models" and that "value—what the customer eventually gets—was a back-seat discussion." He also noted that the unearned stock market success of these companies was facilitated by public markets that were "gullible and ready to buy equity in half-baked, or even quarter-baked, 'companies.'" Since then, Forrester—and others—have gone on to predict that most retailers that operate entirely on the Internet will be out of business shortly.

Bursting the Dotcom Bubble

So what went wrong? For one thing, most dotcoms never really made a clear case that they were delivering real value to customers in the first place. In fact, many dotcom companies went out into the market with business plans that were poorly thought out. Of course, lots of companies have done that over the years. The difference was that the dotcoms were still able to attract immense amounts of capital from the stock market even though they didn't have a proven track record of profitability. That's something that never happened before on such a large scale. In the early days of the Internet boom, investors were willing to forego the usual criteria because they believed that something new was going on. They didn't want to miss out. It was kind of like the mid-1960s in the wake of The Beatles. Record companies were willing to sign any and every long-haired British band they could find. A few got lucky, finding the likes of The Rolling Stones and The Kinks, but a lot more wound up with Freddie and the Dreamers and similar bands.

Here's the point, though: The dotcom business model was *never* a huge success. The valuations that the markets gave to dotcom companies were a distortion based largely on simple supply and demand. There were not enough genuine dotcom companies, such as *Amazon.com* is, to accommodate all of the investor dollars in the marketplace. The business press, which has never had a particularly good understanding of technology, was too superficial to distinguish between the performance of dotcom stocks and that of dotcom companies. One article after another offered analysis that offered reasons why dotcom companies were going to be so successful, when there was little objective evidence that such was going to be the case. As a result, businesspeople, who followed the phenomenon on the press and didn't want to miss out on a major shift in the marketplace, were left with the impression that online commerce was devastating traditional sales and marketing approaches.

Lessons for Sales and Marketing Executives

My objective here is not to provide you with a historical analysis of how the dotcom bubble burst. What I'm trying to do is to get you to question some assumptions you might have been operating under for the last few years. Specifically, if you've been thinking that it's time to close your sales offices, fire your field-based salespeople, or shut down your retail stores, you need to think again. Let me give you a basic rule of thumb: All other things being equal, it's much better to have a physical presence in your marketplace than to not have one.

Don't misunderstand me. There are a lot of great things that you can do on the Web. In fact, much of the rest of this book is devoted to describing them in detail. But it's important for you to not lose sight of the fact that your existing sales and marketing channels bring real value—unique value—to your relationship with your customers.

Let's begin with the fact that a physical presence in your marketplace carries with it a credibility that's extremely difficult to achieve otherwise. In a retail situation, for example, a store means that your customers know that they have someplace to go if there's a problem. A store is perceived to be real and substantial, not virtual or ephemeral.

A store can also give your customers a greater sense of control than they might have when shopping on the Web. (This can cut both ways, though. There's another aspect of control that you'll learn about in Chapter 9.) A retail store also means that your customers don't have to wonder about delivery issues. The product goes directly from you to them. Period. They don't have to worry about searching for a phone number or wait for who-knows-how-long on hold in order to get a problem addressed.

Credibility and a sense of control on the part of your customers are concerns in the area of business-to-business sales, too. When it comes to achieving credibility with your business customers, there are very few things you can do that are more effective than dispatching an obviously well-qualified sales professional. It conveys the message that you're going to be there if there's a problem in much the same way that the presence of a retail store does to a consumer.

In addition, your business customers feel more in control when you provide them with a single focal point for accountability. Even when you provide them with points of contact for service and support issues, most business customers will use their salesperson as their default contact for any and all interactions with your company. In fact, this is a legendary source of complaint in most sales organizations. The truth is that it just reflects the nature of how our customers want to work with us.

Although I want to stay focused on customer benefits right now, it's worth mentioning that face-to-face selling, whether it's done in a store or by a salesperson in the field, has some distinct benefits for you, too. As a seller, you have the ability to design the sales environment and direct the sales situation. You also have the ability to react to questions, objections, or hesitation on the part of your customer. You can more directly influence the direction of the sale. These are not insignificant advantages.

The Social Element of Commerce

In addition to credibility and control, there's another important reason why you need your stores, sales offices, and salespeople. Although you probably haven't given it much thought, there is an important social element involved in all of your interactions with your customers that is unique and irreplaceable.

Think about a Saturday afternoon at a typical shopping mall. You don't have to look too closely to see that there's a lot going on besides shopping. People are there to get out of the house, to see their friends and neighbors, and to be seen by their friends and neighbors.

Clearly, though, what the best retail merchants understand very well is that, in the midst of the social interaction, a great deal of shopping takes place. You've heard this before, but it's true nevertheless: The shopping mall has replaced the town square as the focal point for all sorts of social interaction.

This social element goes beyond teenagers hanging out with their friends. You can see it in bookstores, at cosmetics counters, and in clothing stores. Shoppers will spend time looking for input from a sales clerk, or asking that clerk's opinion about how a particular suit looks.

The same basic principle of the importance of social interaction applies when it comes to business sales, although it usually manifests itself somewhat differently. An obvious example is a salesperson spending an afternoon on the golf course with a client, but there are all kinds of sales interactions that demonstrate this principle. Taking a client out to lunch or to an afternoon baseball game fall into this category. In fact, even a plain, vanilla sales call at a client's office usually has a social element to it. After all, don't the best salespeople spend more time than they really need to shooting the breeze with clients about how Tiger Woods is likely to do next weekend or who's going to the Superbowl?

It would be difficult to overstate the importance of the social factor. Successful marketers learn two things very early in their careers. The first is that people buy from people they like. The second is that customers almost always buy for emotional reasons and only afterwards justify their decisions logically. Social interaction first establishes and then strengthens the emotional investment that your customers have in doing business with you. (If you want to learn more about how these principles can be applied to your business, check out *Influenceatwork.com,* a Web site that's based on the groundbreaking work of psychologist Robert Cialdini.)

Commerce as Entertainment

Another aspect of selling and marketing that is difficult to duplicate on the Web is entertainment. Make no mistake about it: Entertainment is a vital ingredient in all different kinds of sales and marketing situations, far more than you might realize. Consider just a few examples:

@   The end cap display at your local supermarket featuring a perfectly shaped pyramid of Pepsi cans stacked all the way to the ceiling.

@   A new product roll-out by Microsoft featuring a film of Bill Gates and Steve Ballmer in a parody of one of Volkswagen's television commercials.

@   A waiter at Ruth's Chris Steakhouse in a perfectly starched white shirt, bringing you a New York Sirloin that is sizzling so loudly, you can hear it from across the dining room.

@   An exhibition booth at an industrial trade show where a basketball hoop is set up and you have three chances to sink a free throw to win a $100 product voucher.

@   The aisles of a Sam's Club outlet on a Saturday morning where associates are cooking various foods for you to sample.

@   The salesperson for a commercial realtor giving an elaborate, multimedia PowerPoint presentation on a planned office complex to a prospective corporate tenant.

All of these are instances of sales and marketing situations that feature an important entertainment component. Savvy marketers are becoming more and more aware of the importance of adding an element of entertainment to every business interaction. Christopher Lochhead, the Chief Marketing Officer at Scient, validated this premise recently when he was describing to me some research that his firm had done on what motivates people to buy from a particular vendor. He explained:

Basically what we discovered is that price is not a big motivator for people. Convenience, although it's important in some demographics, is not that important. Do you know what the number one most important thing that came back from our analysis was? The most important thing about the buying experience was how entertaining it is. In other words, consumers are asking, "How much fun is this?"

It's not that it's impossible to be entertaining on the Web. In fact, the research that Lochhead described to me was designed to find ways to do exactly that. It's just that there are more opportunities to do it in the context of a face-to-face encounter. And there are more ways to do it in a way that is engaging and compelling.

Moving Beyond Conventional Thinking About the Internet

Some of these ideas in this chapter may be at odds with Internet market research you've seen, either from studies that you've conducted yourself with your customers or from third party research you've read. Although it's usually true that you ignore specific customer input at your own peril, it's also true that customers are not always consciously aware of all of the factors that ultimately motivate their behavior. That's worth considering if you've ever been tempted by research that says that customers aren't influenced significantly by face-to-face contact.

David Pottruck, ex-CEO of Charles Schwab, is a guy who ought to know about these things. His former company's online presence, *Schwab.com,* is one of the most successful brokerage sites in the industry. David described a fascinating example of how this all works in his book, *Clicks and Mortar:*

A great paradox in marketing (and one of the most difficult skills to develop) is how you learn to listen to customers, to hear what they can't say directly, and then select what to believe and act on. The "selective listening" is a way of listening and not listening at the same time....We've had many successes, and avoided many disasters, from this kind of selective listening at Schwab. In fact, whenever we do market research—and we've been doing this for 15 years— we ask people, "How important is having a local branch office?" It actually scores fairly low, maybe seventh or eighth on a customer's typical wish list. Yet every time we open a local office, we double the new business we get in that community....Our success with local offices particularly flies in the face of conventional Internet wisdom.

The importance of in-person interaction persists today, and there's every reason to believe that it will continue to persist into the foreseeable future. In a recent issue of *Fortune,* John Sullivan, the Chief Financial Officer of Trans World Entertainment, put it best. He was commenting on the fact that retail outlets for items such as books and CDs continue to flourish in the face of online competition. He said simply, "People like to shop." And that just about says it all.

Sure, there will be a few companies that carve out a position in the marketplace based on a pure Internet presence. But there will be relatively few of them. It's worth noting that the best of those companies still manage to incorporate some elements of human interaction into the equation. Take a close look at *Amazon.com,* for example. It's true that Amazon has limited its shopping and ordering experience to online interaction. But, in contrast to less savvy Web players, it also provides an 800 number that is staffed with customer service representatives seven days a week, 24 hours a day. (If you don't think that customer service at that level is a marketing investment, let me suggest that you think again. What Amazon understands is that every point of contact between the company and its customers is a sales and/or marketing opportunity. And, whether you've thought about it that way or not, the same thing is true for your company.)

The bottom line of all of this is simple. One of the biggest problems with a pure dotcom approach to sales and marketing is this: It's not that either of those things can't be somehow accomplished online. It's that, when you come right down to it, there are simply some things that are much better when they're done in person.

There's one more reason, though, why your sales and marketing plan needs to extend beyond the Internet. Despite all the hype, the truth is that the Internet does not deliver customers. I'll explain what you can do about that in Chapter 3.

Barton A. Weitz

Barton A. Weitz is Chairman of the Marketing Department, the JCPenney Eminent Scholar Chair, and Executive Director of the Center for Retailing Education and Research at the University of Florida. Professor Weitz's research interests focus on electronic retailing and the development of long-term relationships between firms in a channel of distribution (retailers and vendors), firms and their employees, and salespeople and their customers.

Colombo: In the future, what is the relationship going to be between physical stores and the Web presence of the companies running those stores?

Weitz: Most of this electronic retailing is going to be dominated by store-based retailers. They'll use those stores to perform a certain set of activities and use the Web to do other activities. Now, they'll sell over the Web and they'll sell things in the stores, but they'll use the Web to support what goes on in the store. Take Home Depot. You'd be able to get on the Web and say, "Well, if I want to replace my bathtub, what do I need to get?" And you might send an order in and go by the store and pick up this kit of things that you need, or find out whether it's available in the store, or if you need to order it long distance.

Colombo: Are different products or different product categories more appropriate to one place or another?

Weitz: There are some products that are probably more easily sold on the Web than in stores, but the key is not whether it has "touch and feel attributes" versus "look and see." The key is whether you can provide enough information from a particular source to make people feel confident in their decision. For example, who would ever buy perfume on the Web? You can't smell it. And that's its biggest attribute. I have no problem buying a branded product on the Web, because I know it's going to be the exact same product as what's available in the store. A brand name provides you with confidence that you can get exactly what you want on the Web. So, branded products would probably sell much better on the Web than generic or unfamiliar ones.

Colombo: There are two issues there: the branding of the products and the branding of the retailer.

Weitz: But they're both critical. One of the inherited advantages of store-based retailers is that they have very good brand names—Neiman Marcus, Saks Fifth Avenue, Bloomingdale's—but I'm scared to death to go to *perfume.net* or *perfumenet.com*. More because I don't know if, in fact, they delivered something that is, say, out of date. How do I know? That's why branding of a retailer's name is critical on the Web.

Colombo: Another factor in this Web-versus-store scenario is the logistics of delivery. You can ship a book relatively inexpensively. Products with other form factors wouldn't have the same low cost.

Weitz: It's a big issue. That one mile from that store to your home has a huge cost. And as a percentage of the overall cost, that cost is going be much greater for things like lumber than it's going to be for diamonds. And that's why dotcom companies are now realizing the importance of distribution. When many dotcoms started out they would say, "Well, I'll outsource the distribution. I'll give it to these wholesalers to distribute." But you can't trust the wholesalers to do it, because if they lose a customer because of bad delivery, the customer is gone forever. So, now the dotcoms are building warehouses. They've realized that they have to have efficient delivery.

Colombo: Is it likely that an entire product category, such as books, will eventually find the bulk of its business on the Web, because there's such a good fit between that category and what the Web has to offer?

Weitz: There are still so many situations in which people want instant gratification. It's still fun to shop in a store. It's still fun to have a cup of coffee and look at your book in Barnes & Noble. And in the United States, stores are so accessible. I can see the Internet accounting for maybe 25 percent of retail sales in certain categories. Even if it takes 10 percent, a lot of stores are going to be closed.

Colombo: Are there any guidelines in terms of what works better on the Web and what works better in the stores, regarding whether a product is differentiated or a commodity?

Weitz: On some of these things what you have to think through is the supply and demand. You don't need as much information about undifferentiated products. On the other hand, those are also the least profitable yet most price sensitive things to sell. The real problem is having a branded product sold by multiple Web sites when you can comparison shop so easily and buy at the lowest price. We have search engines to do that. What's going to happen is that you're going to find much more emphasis on private label merchandising. It's unique, so that I don't have to give price comparisons.

An executive at Burdines told me that its gift baskets consist of branded products, but it bundles them so they really can't be compared with somebody else's gift basket. So you bundle products and services together for multiple products in such a way that it would be difficult to compare them across retailers. That's a subtle—and critical—issue when it comes to making money.

Colombo: Is this why differentiating a product can be so important?

Weitz: Right. You have to find a way to differentiate your product. Amazon can differentiate its books because it offers one-click shopping and suggestions of things that you may prefer based on its history of you. So maybe you're paying more, but, you'll say, "I can go to a search engine and find this book for a buck cheaper, but do I want to spend the time to do it?"

Colombo: One of things that I believe in is creating a coherence between what you do on the Web and what you do in the stores. Should there be Web specials? Should there be a price that you can get on the Web but not in the store? Or, conversely, should there be store specials (something that you can get if you walk in the store that you couldn't get if you were shopping on the Web site)?

Weitz: You probably *should* have differences because, ultimately, you'll find some people who would prefer shopping in one mode versus another mode for different types of products. You're going to find more special promotions on the Web, because you'll know who's going to buy them and who's not. Let me give an example. If you have seamless integration between stores and the Internet, so that you know a customer's complete history, why not make that available to a sales associate at the cash register? Why shouldn't this sales associate have a little thing that pops up at the cash register that says, "Mary Jones is checking out right now. Mary's bought this, this, and this, so why don't you offer her this?" Why don't retailers do that? They do it on the Web.

Colombo: I was also thinking about it in the other direction. Does it make sense to capture information at the store and send an e-mail that says, "Thanks for coming in and buying those pants this afternoon."?

Weitz: Absolutely. And in fact, most customer information is going to be caught in the store. So you could e-mail a customer when his alteration is finished. Or you could e-mail a customer who came in looking for a size 42 jacket if you didn't have one in stock to say that you just got new stock. Or, if you have excess inventory in 44 longs, you can go through the database, find everybody who is a 44 long and—

Colombo: —and send them an e-mail.

Weitz: Once you start thinking of these things, there are just millions of these synergies.

Colombo: In both directions: from the Web to the store, and from the store to the database out to the Web. But do you still believe that the companies that have a physical presence in the community ultimately are going to have a huge advantage over companies that are just virtual?

Weitz: Yes. One important reason is that the cost to get a customer if you're a store-based retailer is a third of what it is if you're a pure Internet retailer. The store's physical presence is free advertising. It creates the brand image.

Colombo: Some companies have gone out of their way to segregate their e-businesses from their brick-and-mortar businesses. Are there any reasons why that makes sense to do?

Weitz: It's purely a financial ploy. I don't think it makes any sense to do that.

Colombo: Mostly what we've talked about has to do with companies that have, probably, a national retail presence, or at least a regional presence. Any thoughts about a mom-and-pop retailer, relative to what makes sense for them to be doing on the Web?

Weitz: There's still a big opportunity for these mom-and-pops because the Internet has worldwide access, and that broadens your customer base. But it has lots of other benefits, too: providing information, personalization, interactivity, that kind of thing. And local businesses can explore those. Those local businesses that have good reputations in a particular area and have a loyal set of customers can communicate with their customers over the Internet and they can sell stuff. They might have to set up a distribution system, but it might be worth it.

Colombo: Are there businesses for whom it doesn't make any sense to be thinking about having a presence on the Web?

Weitz: If you're a retailer, the Web *always* benefits you. It doesn't make much sense for companies like Proctor & Gamble to spend lots of money on the Web, because they always have to sell their products through a retailer. Selling products and services is what's going to financially support any Web business; the chances of Proctor & Gamble or other packaged goods companies being able to sell things to people is minimal. So, they're using the Web for brand building. They have a site that will tell you how to get dirt and spots off clothing and recommend you use Tide. They'll find out eventually that has some benefit, but it's not worth that much.

Colombo: What about the social component of going into a physical location, talking with people? What about the kinds of things that happen in stores that can never happen on the Web?

Weitz: People go shopping for lots of different reasons. They want to see what's new, they want to get out of the house, they want to be less bored, they want to be around people. Those experiences are not really captured and satisfied on the Web. Stores are very good at providing social experiences—this sort of theatrical experience of retail entertainment; a lot of stores are evolving into being demonstration centers for stuff you'll buy over the Web. So you'll see places where you go in there and swing golf clubs and see what feels good in your hands and then actually it's fulfilled on the Web. Or there's a limited amount of merchandise actually in the store.

Colombo: For the retail executives who have dipped their toes in the water on the Web, are at the brochureware level— in other words, their sites just say, "Here's how wonderful we are! Please visit our stores!"—and are looking to take the next step. What direction would you point them in?

Weitz: Take a *big* step. In other words, putting your toe in the water has a chance of leaving you behind. What you have to do is make a big investment and do it first rate. And then you have to put the systems behind it. The systems are critical. It's not about making a pretty Web site. It's about actually being able to provide customer service—do the fulfillment, track the orders. You have to make a big investment to put those systems in, because that's what's going to create the satisfied customers in the long run.

Chapter 3

You Can't Count on the Web to Deliver Customers

S uper Bowl XXXIV was played on January 30, 2000 in Atlanta between the St. Louis Rams and the Tennessee Titans. It was more exciting than most Super Bowls, with the outcome in the balance until the very last play of the game. Although the game itself was the focal point of water cooler conversations the following day, it was the advertising that people talked about for weeks afterwards.

What caused all the buzz? It was the fact that the program seemed to be dominated by ads for dotcom companies. The previous year's Super Bowl featured the first trickle of dotcom ads (notably, some clever ads from *Monster.com,* an online job search site), but by the time Super Bowl XXXIV aired, that trickle had turned into a flood. In addition to *Monster.com,* viewers were bombarded by ads from companies including:

@   *Autotrader.com*

@   *Computer.com*

@   *Etrade.com*

@   *Webmd.com*

@   *Kforce.com*

@   *Lifeminders.com*

@   *Netpliance.com*

@   *Onmoney.com*

@   *Ourbeginning.com*

@   *Pets.com*

Other advertisers that were Internet-related but not necessarily pure dotcom plays (such as *The Wall Street Journal* Interactive Edition and Oxygen Media) rounded out the collection. The final tally revealed that 17 of the 36 companies that sponsored the Super Bowl were related to the Internet in one way or another.

The glut of dotcom companies that were lined up to advertise on the Super Bowl was so great that it was reportedly the single biggest factor in driving up the cost of a single 30-second spot to a record $2.2 million. One of the companies, *Computer.com,* ran three 30-second spots at a reported cost of something in the neighborhood of $3.5 million. That figure by itself is amazing enough when you consider that it didn't even buy enough time to cook an egg. It becomes downright staggering when you realize that it represented more than 60 percent of the company's total funding! The presence of *Ourbeginning.com* was, in some respects, even more amazing. The company is basically on online stationery store with specialty items such as birth announcements and wedding invitations! (Evidently, it was targeting all the brides-to-be and expectant mothers who watch the Super Bowl!)

High-tech Infatuation · With Low-tech Marketing

The Super Bowl was certainly an excessive example, but it was definitely not an aberration. In fact, the most well-known and well-respected names on the Internet are voracious consumers of traditional advertising media. In fact, from 1998 to 1999, the ad budgets for the top 10 dotcom advertisers more than doubled. Companies such as E*trade, Ameritrade, *Amazon.com,* and America Online can regularly be found advertising in traditional media (radio and television).

In fact, the appetite of the most cutting-edge dotcom companies for marketing exposure even extends to the least cutting-edge media you can think of. For example, the next time you're in California, spend a half hour or so driving up and down Highway 101 between San Jose and San Francisco. You'll see billboard after billboard for Web sites that you've almost certainly never heard of before.

Another great example of this trend showed up in my mailbox a few months ago. It was a blue Val-Pak envelope, a marketing device that, like billboards, is about as traditional and low-tech as you can get. Blazoned across the back of the envelope was the question, "Do you Yahoo?"

All of this is interesting and even amusing, but it has real significance for you as you develop and refine your marketing plan. You have probably been told that the Internet is a great vehicle for getting customers. But here's the question you ought to be asking yourself: If dotcom companies are spending their marketing budgets on television, radio, and other "offline" media instead of online promotions, then what do they know that I don't?

That's a darn good question, especially when you consider the fact that the marketing managers of these companies are more familiar with the Internet and its capabilities than anyone else on the planet! The answer is simple and straightforward. The Internet is not usually the best vehicle for attracting new customers. In other words, if your objective is to put lots of new prospects into the top of your prospect pipeline, then you ought to take a lesson from the hippest, hottest high-tech companies in the world. You need to extend your marketing mix beyond the Internet.

"Wait a minute," I hear you saying. "What about the search engines? Won't customers who are looking for my product or service find me on the search engines?" The answer is that some of them will, but the numbers are not likely to be significant enough to make a big difference.

First of all, a great deal of the searching that takes place on the Web is not being conducted by buyers looking for vendors. Among the most popular search terms on the Web, here are a few perennial favorites:

@ MP3

@ Sex

@ Computer

@ Jennifer Lopez

@ Music

@ Britney Spears

@ Java

If your Web site is likely to turn up when those search terms are entered into a search engine, then you're in good shape. Chances are, though, that the nature of the products or services that you're selling is not represented on this list.

Another problem with search engines is that, in spite of what you might hear, it is difficult, if not quite impossible, to manipulate your search engine rankings in a meaningful way. For one thing, in many cases, positioning on a particular search engine is basically a form of paid advertising. In other words, companies buy their positioning for particular search terms. Beyond that, most experts agree that once you get beyond the first page or two of search results, you're out of luck. Unless you're operating in a very narrowly defined niche (or, of course, unless people are searching specifically for you or your company), the chances of your turning up in the top 20 or so listings is slim indeed.

Greg Renker is the CEO of Guthy-Renker, one of the world's largest direct-response television companies with annual sales in excess of $350 million. (Direct-response companies are more credible about this sort of thing than other companies because they don't guess; they measure.) Here's what he had to say about his company's experience with efforts to increase its rankings in the search engines:

> *We also have identified that as much time we've spent trying to maximize search engine optimization—meaning causing our brand names to appear highest in the ranking of the various search engines, so when people type in categories, whether its hair growth or acne, they would go to our product—so far, all of our information indicates that, from a sales point of view, that's borderline irrelevant. What counts is the promotion of the URL, along with the brand, in all of our mainstream direct response advertising. That's where our sales are coming from.*

Tactics for Getting Hits

Obviously, though, the goal of driving traffic to your Web site is an important one. There are lots of productive things that you can do from a sales and marketing standpoint once you get prospective customers to visit you on the Web. I'm not saying that driving Web traffic is not worthwhile. What I am saying is that, with a couple of important exceptions, most of your best opportunities to drive Web traffic are not found on the Web itself.

One important thing you can do, if possible, is to create a congruence between you company's name and/or product and your Web address. This works in a couple of ways. One is that potential customer who is vaguely aware of your company will often try to find you by typing in your company name as a Web address to see what happens. If you were looking for McDonald's, for example, your first inclination wouldn't be to go to a search engine to find it. You'd simply try trying in *Mcdonalds.com* and see what happens. (An ideal tactic is to align your company name and Web address with a word that represents an entire category or industry. *Pets.com* is a great example of this approach. The problem, of course, is that most desirable dotcom domain names are long since gone. By the time you read this, however, it's likely that there will be several new top level domains available.)

Contrast that approach with the positioning of a company such as *Fogdog.com*. No, they don't sell rainwear. And they don't sell pet products. They sell sporting goods. (A group of people sat around a conference table one day and decided that naming the company "Fogdog" was a good idea. Amazing.)

You can (and often should) take the principle of making the name of your company do double marketing duty one step further by actually building dotcom into your company name. In that way, all of your marketing across all of the media you use will automatically direct potential customers to your Web site, allowing every marketing dollar you spend to do double duty. For example, whenever *Priceline.com* advertises, every mention of the company name automatically customers to its Web site. Public Radio, on the other hand, is not as well-positioned with its retail catalog company. The name of the company and its catalog is *Wireless*. However, the Web site of the same name, *Wireless.com,* belongs to the wireless communications industry. As a result, the catalog company must simultaneously promote its catalog name (*Wireless*) and its Web site (*WirelessToo.com*). It would be far better off to bite the bullet and come up with a name that it can own both in print and on the Web.

You have, no doubt, noticed that the title of this book adheres to this principle. This is a great example of how the principle can work. (And, perhaps, this book found its way into your hands as a result of its success!) The title of the book mirrors a Web site of the same name. As a result, whenever the book title is mentioned in a book review, on a radio or television program, or in an article, a potential reader who is interested in the subject immediately knows where to go on the Web to get more information. Every promotional initiative then becomes doubly effective and, as the author, I am free to talk to interviewers about the book without having to shoehorn into the conversation the obligatory but annoying phrase, "You know, if your viewers want more information, they can visit our Web site...."

The next part of your Web traffic strategy should be to make sure that your Web address appears on every single piece of printed matter that your company produces. Examples of where your Web address ought to be listed include (but are certainly not limited to):

@   Letterhead.

@   Envelopes.

@   Advertising pieces.

@   Business cards.

@   Flyers.

@   Invoices and account statements.

@   Checks.

@   Catalogs.

@   Promotional materials.

@   Press releases.

@   Cash register receipts.

In other words: everywhere. Anyone who receives a piece of paper from your company—for any reason whatsoever—ought to be receiving your Web address right along with it. Putting this tactic into practice doesn't cost you anything, so any sales impact you get, even if it's incremental, will have been achieved at a net cost of zero.

Let's look at Guthy-Renker's experience according to Greg Renker:

> *We simply promote the Internet the same way we do our 800 number—no more, no less. Wherever our 800 number appears, our URL addresses for our products appear....We do not appear to have any diminishment of calls into the 800 number, as measured. We do have an obvious increase in people who order our brand off the Web.*

New Life for an Old Approach

Earlier in this chapter, I mentioned that dotcom companies in the Silicon Valley area were using billboard advertising. This is probably an ineffective approach unless the name of your Web site is exceptionally memorable. That's because very few people are going to take the time to jot down a Web address while they're driving. These companies may think they're making an impression, but if the company is not already a household name, a brief impression won't easily translate into some kind of action on the part of potential customers. As a result, it's a questionable investment. Interestingly enough, though, a different kind of low-tech marketing tactic might not only help your company make the same kind of impression for your company and Web site, but it can also be there to help your customers take action to follow up.

The tactic I'm referring to is the use of novelty items. You know the kinds of things I'm talking about—inexpensive gift and give-away items that you leave on a client's desk at the end of a sales call or that you hand out at trade shows and other similar events. Examples of novelties would be golf tees, paperweights, rubber hand exercisers, keychains, T-shirts, and so forth. Before the proliferation of the Internet, I was hardly enthusiastic about this kind of marketing expenditure. It didn't seem as though you could accomplish enough with the limited space available on most novelties to make them effective to use. It was possible to include your company's name, phone number, and maybe a brief marketing message.

From a marketing standpoint, you couldn't ask a novelty item to do too much. And what it *could* do hardly seemed worth it. With the Internet, though, the same brief marketing message can now be coupled with your Web address. The ability to keep your Web address in close proximity to your customer so that it's right there when he or she is surfing around on the Web changes the marketing equation by dramatically increasing the potential payoff. Obviously, novelties are not going to be the foundation of your marketing program, but if they're used judiciously, they can be a valuable adjunct. And I'm very confident that they'll deliver a bigger payoff for you in terms of driving traffic to your Web site than billboards on the side of the highway.

A Couple of Very Targeted Tactics to Use Online

I mentioned earlier that there are a couple of specific online tactics that can be extremely effective when it comes to driving traffic to your Web site. They are both variations on a single theme: Target your marketing at specific groups of prospects who are likely to have an interest in your product or service.

The first tactic is to arrange for reciprocating links with other Web sites that offer noncompeting products and services to the same group of customers. For example, let's say that your company has just signed an exclusive deal to import and distribute a new line of premium, handmade cigars from the Dominican Republic. Your target customer is pretty easy to identify. You're primarily looking for upscale, male consumers. Think for a minute about what else that particular consumer is likely to purchase. A little bit of guesswork and a little bit of market research tell you that your target prospect is likely to drink single malt scotch. Your course of action, then, would be to identify a company that sells single malt scotch. The two companies would then link to each other's Web sites.

This approach has a couple of distinct advantages. You can often use this approach with little or no cost, because the arrangement is reciprocal. Each site is linking to the other. The other advantage is that, depending on how the reciprocating links are designed and positioned, each site is taking advantage of the credibility that the other site has with its customers. It is a variation of the endorsed mailings strategy that is used in the direct marketing industry.

The other related tactic is to take this idea a step further and to compensate the referring site for any sales that are made to customers that link from its site to yours. Unlike banner advertising, where you are ostensibly paying for impressions (an approach that has lost credibility dramatically as Web surfers have gotten amazingly skilled at ignoring ads), this approach allows you to only pay for results. And working on the Web gives you the ability to implement technology that allows you to keep track of everything easily.

One of the best examples of this approach is also, in my opinion, one of the most underappreciated marketing success stories that the Web has to offer: *Amazon.com*'s affiliate program is a marketing initiative that operates through thousands of independent Web sites. The idea is simple. Web site operators offer books for sale on their sites. The orders are placed and fulfilled through Amazon, which compensates the site operators with a percentage of each sale. It is a situation in which everyone wins. The site operator is able to offer books that are of value to his or her customers without having to invest in inventory or worry about the operational hassles of fulfillment. Amazon, meanwhile, extends its reach into the marketplace tremendously and only has to pay when an actual sale is made.

Are there Web sites that sell to the same sorts of customers that also buy what you sell? If so, your products or services might compliment what they're doing in a way that would allow for an affiliate-type of arrangement. Those sorts of situations are out there and they offer tremendous value for both parties.

Another Advantage of the Web

If you want to maximize your efforts at driving Web traffic over time, you need to have a clear handle on where your visitors and customers are coming from. Once you know where your visitors are coming from—once you know which of your promotional efforts was successful in driving traffic to your site—you can then do more of the same (or, at least, do something similar) to drive still more traffic in the future. This kind of analysis is difficult in other business environments. In a retail store, for example, it's not always easy to know where your customers are coming from or what got them there in the first place.

One of the great things about Web technology, though, is that this type of information is relatively easy to get. You should be making it a point to get and analyze as much of it as you can.

If you're a sales or marketing executive at a large company, then your Webmaster will be able to produce reports with all the information you need to make intelligent marketing decisions. If you're a smaller company, though, the company that is hosting your Web site can provide you with the same information. In many instances, it's already part of your Web hosting service. If it's not, it's likely to be available for an additional charge that's nominal.

For example, one of the Web sites that my company operates is located with a Web hosting company that offers traffic analysis produced by a company called *WebTrends.com,* one of the leading vendors in that field. I am able to get regular reports on such topics as:

@ Top referring sites.

@ Top referring URLs.

@ Top search engines.

@ Top search keywords.

@ Most active organizations.

With this information, I know exactly where the visitors to this site are coming from. (By the way, these reports offer all kinds of other interesting and important information beyond what you need to know to drive more traffic. For instance, you can find out how much time the average visitor spends on your site and which page a visitor is most likely to be on when he or she exits.) It would be extremely difficult, maybe even impossible, to market this site in a meaningful way without access to this kind of information. If your company has a Web site, this information exists and is available to you. If you haven't reviewed it yet, make sure you get your hands on it right away.

Now that we've examined some ideas for driving traffic to your Web site, we're going to start to figure out exactly what it is that you want your Web site to accomplish and how to coordinate your Web activities with what you're doing in your stores, in your sales offices, or out in the field with your salespeople. In other words, Chapter 4 is going to guide you through the process of redefining your business in a wired world.

Redefining Your Business for a Wired World

A long time ago, I heard someone say that the definition of a fanatic is someone who redoubles his efforts even after he's forgotten his objective. If that's the case, then I think it's fair to say that much of the effort that's been made by businesses over the last couple of years to get online has been somewhat fanatical. The kindest thing that can be said is that businesses are scrambling to get something done without being entirely clear on why they're doing it, or even what they're trying to achieve. Amazingly, it's not just smaller companies that are guilty here. Some of the country's largest, most well-known companies have obviously spent enormous amounts of money on Web sites that are not doing much of anything.

The power and versatility of the Internet mean that there are a number of different things you can do with a Web site. The two questions you need to constantly ask yourself in order to make sense of it all are: What are my business objectives, and how can the Internet help me achieve them?

The underlying point here—one that seems to have escaped so many otherwise bright people—is that being on the Internet, in and of itself, does not constitute a business objective. Over the last few years, all sorts of businesses in many different industries have been bombarded with the questions, "What is your Internet strategy? What is your e-business strategy?" These questions miss the point entirely. More than anything else, they divert the attention of sales and marketing executives from the real issues: capturing customers and making sales. Developing an "Internet strategy" doesn't make any more sense than developing a "telephone strategy" or a "fax strategy." Each one of those is a tool that can be used as a way to achieve one or more business objectives. From a sales and marketing standpoint, that should mean doing something to acquire or create value for customers. Just as the phone or the fax can, the Internet can be used skillfully or clumsily. But it's not a silver bullet; it's just a tool.

Let's start, then, by taking a moment to look at some of the general possibilities that are available to you as you consider what your sales and marketing objectives are for your Web site. We'll look at them in a more or less ascending order of value.

Provide Information About Your Company, Products, and Services

This is the logical place to begin for most businesses. If your Web site doesn't go beyond this level of functionality, it falls into a category that Web cognoscenti disdainfully refer to as brochureware. Don't be intimidated. This may be a perfectly appropriate level of functionality for you, at least for the time being.

Even if your Web site stays at this level of functionality, there are a few things that you should keep in mind. The most important is that when it comes to providing information about your company, the most important information you can possibly provide is a way to contact you. It should be a no-brainer for customers to find out how to contact you. Incredibly, many Web sites either make no provisions for customer contact or they do it in a way that is so difficult to figure out that the practical effect is the same as not doing it at all.

Pepsi Cola's Web site, *Pepsi.com,* is a case in point. There's nothing on the home page that even suggests that it's possible to contact the company. You've got to navigate over to the FAQ (Frequently Asked Questions) page before you come across an e-mail link to contact the company. Even then, the link is to the Webmaster and it's apparently only for people who are having technical problems with the site. (Using that link, I sent an e-mail several months ago asking if the company had any plans to offer its Cherry Pepsi product in a diet version. I still haven't heard back.)

Another important point about offering product information is to remember that the Web removes the kinds of constraints that you have when you're communicating information about your product in other media. You're not working with a limited amount of space you can afford as you might be in print advertising, radio, or television. And you don't have to worry about printing costs that might be a concern if you were printing catalogs or brochures. On the Web, you've got as much space as you need or want to describe each one of your products. This being the case, you need to keep in mind this truism from marketing expert Dan Kennedy: The more you tell, the more you'll sell.

Prospective customers who are interested in your products want to know more about them, not less, before making a purchasing decision. You can probably count on getting some pushback on this point from the people who are designing your Web site. They will tell you that including a lot of product information can interfere with the aesthetics of your Web site. The appropriate response to that argument is, "Baloney!"

It's a variation of the same kind of thing that you hear from ad agencies when it comes to traditional media. They want you to stick with entertaining, aesthetically pleasing ads. Lots of "white space" in print ads. Clever, catchy hooks on radio and television. Those kinds of ads, you'll hear, are the ones that win all the awards. The problem is that there is no evidence whatsoever that these award-winning ads actually sell any product. And there's plenty of evidence that they don't. Taco Bell's famous Chihuahua is one of the latest in a long, long series of award-winning ads that have failed to deliver any sales results for the companies who are paying the bills.

The same principle is becoming all too commonplace on the Web. Never forget that your objective is not to design a site that looks good, is cool, or employs the latest and greatest technology. Your objective should always be to sell more or to somehow address the needs of your customers.

Although you certainly don't want to deploy technology for its own sake, you also don't want to fail to take advantage of technology that's at your disposal when it comes to showcasing your products. Would a brief video tell the story significantly better than a still picture? Would audio commentary make a big difference? If so, throw them in there. On the Web, there's no reason that you can't.

Become an Information Destination for Prospective Customers

This degree of functionality is one that you should consider if it makes sense to have visitors regularly visiting and/

or returning to your Web site, even when they're not there to buy something or otherwise interact with your company. (By the way, the idea of questioning whether or not it makes sense to encourage people to visit your site without a specific purpose is a bit of a heresy among Web folks. Conventional wisdom, of course, is that you should design a site that gets bookmarked and visited as often as possible. Well, in some situations it makes sense and in some it doesn't. In some situations, needless Web traffic can slow down your site and make it less responsive to those visitors who are there to buy something. It can also force you into maintaining a Web infrastructure that is larger and more expensive than you really need.)

There are two basic premises that undercut this level of functionality. The first is that you can sell advertising. This business model is becoming more and more difficult as "click through" rates for banner advertising plummet. (If you're collecting the e-mail addresses of your visitors, though, and using them judiciously, you are in better shape. For more on this, see Chapter 7.) The other idea is that if visitors come back to your site often enough, sooner or later they'll buy something. Maybe so, but you're certainly going to have to do a lot of work to achieve a tenuous result.

If you're going to become an information destination, then one course of action is to provide so much information that you become a reference resource for prospects. The alternative is to provide timely information and news that is either unavailable elsewhere or is more convenient to get to from your site.

Sports lends itself to this approach. ESPN's Web site, *espn.com,* is a great example of an information destination that provides volumes of reference information along with lots of late-breaking news. Its business model relies on advertising as well as a subscription service for more in depth information that is not available to the casual visitor.

Facilitate Direct Transactions

This is the level of functionality that most people think of when they refer to e-commerce. It means offering products for sale directly on your Web site. This is a fairly straightforward concept, so I won't belabor the obvious. There are a few key points that you need to keep in mind, though.

The first is to make sure that everything about your online ordering system is as bulletproof as possible. That starts with easy and intuitive navigation. Sure, your Web team can whiz around the site effortlessly. You can probably find your way around, too. None of that proves anything. What you need to do is enlist the aid of your mother's older sister in New Rochelle. Have Aunt Esther sit down and try to order a couple of things from your site. That will give you a reality check on how well your site's navigation works. Here's my rule of thumb: If Aunt Esther's not having fun, then your Web team's work isn't done!

Another important consideration here is making sure that your Web transactions aren't islands of data, isolated from the rest of your company's information systems. In Chapter 6, we'll examine in depth the principle of integrating all of your sales and marketing channels, including your Web site, but this point is so important that it's worth discussing here as well. Your customers don't care about the architecture of your internal information systems. They aren't interested in all the administrative reasons why online orders need to be handled separately from orders placed in your stores. They just want to know what's going on with the order they placed. Any employee who comes into contact with your customers—from your salespeople in your stores to customer service people in the field—ought to be able to tell them.

This is one of those things that sounds perfectly reasonable but can be extremely difficult to achieve. I recently placed an order with a large computer company that touts itself as the prototype of e-business for the new economy (or something like that). After having placed the order online, I asked my assistant to call the company on the phone to get some additional information. She was told that the company's phone sales division wasn't able to access information from the online sales division. She spent a half hour on the phone trying to get the answer to what ought to have been a pretty simple question. Some e-business.

Ongoing Service and Support

This is the top level of Web functionality. It is the level that you reach when your customers are able to interact with you on the Web to get their questions answered and their problems fixed. In many ways, it is ultimate objective of online business.

Although getting to this level is challenging (and not inexpensive from the standpoint of the systems investment you need to make to get there), for many businesses the payoff can be handsome, not only in terms of lowered long-term costs for customer service but also in terms of enhanced customer satisfaction. One word of caution, though. Make sure that you give your customers the option of interacting with you in other ways. Even if your online customer service is terrific, there will always be times when your customers will look for a reassuring voice at the other end of the telephone.

One company I've done business with has carved out a terrific niche in business of renting DVDs through the mail. Its online systems are nicely designed and, for the most part, work as well as can be expected. The company makes a big mistake, though, in not providing for customers who want to pick up the phone for help. (This problem is made worse by the fact that its online customer service staff is not particularly responsive.) My own research (admittedly anecdotal and not scientific) indicates that the company's retention rate would be much higher if it offered a phone support option for customers who need it. The extremely high cost of acquiring new customers means that even a small improvement in customer retention levels would probably more than pay for the associated costs. As we saw in the last chapter, even though *Amazon.com* is the archetype of a dotcom business, it still provides live phone help for those customers who need it. That is a great example to follow.

The Holy Grail

The principles we've examined so far in this chapter apply to doing business online. We've seen in earlier chapters, though, that trying to do business solely online is not a particularly promising approach. On the other hand, the Internet is too powerful to ignore.

The real answer, then—and the underlying principle for virtually every successful business model in the future—is to integrate what you do on the Web with your sales and marketing efforts in your stores, in your sales offices, and by your salespeople out in the field. In fact, a recent study by the Boston Consulting Group and *Shop.org* indicates that in many industries, multichannel players are already enjoying significant advantages in the marketplace.

That's a nifty principle, but I don't want to mislead you. It's going to be a lot tougher than it sounds. For one thing, in many ways, you'll be blazing new trails and trying to navigate uncharted territory. The ideas in this book will provide the general roadmap but you're going to have to fill in many of the particulars yourself.

Of course, those particulars are going to depend on the nature of your unique business. Both the bad news and the good news is that this is not a one-size-fits-all undertaking. It's bad news because it means that there isn't a cookie cutter out there (yet) that you can just apply to your specific business situation.

It's good news, though, because the effort and thought that will be required to make this stuff happen is likely to be beyond what your competitors are willing or able to do. Even if you just get started down this path, you're likely to leave most of your competitors far behind.

Let's take a look, though, at some ideas for capturing customers by integrating your online tactics with your existing sales and marketing efforts in a few general situations:

A Retail Store

The trickiest issues here are going to center on the issue of privacy. We're going to discuss that in depth in Chapter 13, so for the sake of our discussion here, let's operate on the assumption that the privacy question has been successfully addressed. That being the case, think about what you might be able to do if you could relate your customer's in-store experience with his or her online purchasing—in both directions. A world of intriguing possibilities suddenly opens up.

Let's say, for example, that a customer buys an expensive blue pinstripe suit at one of your stores. Subsequent visits to your Web site would feature a personalized start page for that customer with offers for shirts, ties, and accessories that are specifically coordinated to go with his suit. The colors would all be complementary as well as the fashions. For example, you wouldn't offer a shirt with a button-down collar to go with a double-breasted suit.

Or a customer might buy a printer from you online, then stop into one of your retail stores one evening to pick up some paper. Your sales associate would enter in a customer identifier at the cash register and then be alerted to remind the customer that, at average consumption rates, she might save an unnecessary trip back to the store by picking up a replacement ink cartridge.

Dell Computer recently implemented an intriguing variation of this idea in a partnership with Hewlett Packard. When you buy an HP printer with your Dell system and the printer starts to run low on ink, it automatically sends a message to the Dell Web site via the Internet. The correct replacement cartridge is then put into your Dell shopping basket. All you have to do to complete the order is click.

An Outbound Salesforce

Think about a scenario like this: Your salesperson leaves a client's office with an order for four industrial compressors. Later that afternoon, your client receives an e-mail with an order confirmation that allows the client to verify the accuracy of all the elements of the order. The e-mail also contains a link to a Web page where the progress of the in-process order can be monitored.

In the other direction, a prospect might see one of your ads in a trade journal featuring the newest model in your line of earth-moving equipment. He surfs over to your Web site to check out some the specifications of your product and likes what he sees. A button on the product pages says "This Looks Great! I Want to Meet With a Salesperson!" He clicks the button, then fills out a brief form that asks for his name and phone number. Five minutes later, one of your sales assistants is on the phone, offering to schedule a meeting with one of your salespeople for later in the week.

A Professional Practice

The Web can also be the vehicle for your clients or patients to schedule their appointments. Preliminary information can be solicited at this time so that your client or patient spends less time filling out paperwork or answering administrative questions at your office.

After the appointment, a set of follow-up instructions can be made available on a secure Web site. This would lessen any opportunity for misunderstanding. It would also help with compliance issues.

@ @ @

These are just a few ideas about how your existing business can start to incorporate Web technology. We're going to take this to the next level in Chapter 5, where you'll learn how to go beyond just selling products and services. You're going to learn how to start capturing customers!

Capturing Conversations

Christopher Lochhead

●

Christopher Lochhead is the Chief Marketing Officer of Scient, a leading professional services firm that specializes in e-business.

Colombo: Is the combination of supplementing a real-world presence with something on the Internet the winning formula?

Lochhead: Yes. E-business started as departmental initiatives. Then businesses moved from departments to complete enterprises being e-business–available. But there are more start-ups that are complete e-businesses than traditional companies that are. A year ago, we would say things like, "E-business is the business. There won't be a distinction going forward." Some people would argue with you about it. Today, you don't get in the argument. You're seeing more and more companies that are becoming complete e-business or e-business–enabled. As enterprises move down that path, entire markets will become e-business–enabled. And then we move from markets to industries and, ultimately, from industries to economies.

Colombo: Let me draw a distinction. "E-business–enabled" is not saying that we're going to jettison our branch offices or our stores or our sales forces in favor of a pure Internet presence. E-business–enabled is saying that those elements are going to coexist and complement each other. Is that right?

Lochhead: Correct. It's not that we're going to fire our sales force and shut all our branch offices—although we may do *some* of that. But what's clear is that e-business capabilities will, at a minimum, be as important as any other way to which you go to market. And, for many companies, they will be the *primary* way in which they go to market.

Colombo: As you look at a continuum in terms of totally e-business–enabled at one end and very little e-business–enablement at the other end, is there a useful way to evaluate what kinds of industries and what kinds of businesses belong where on that continuum?

Lochhead: There are some that are significantly ahead of the curve, like the big banks and brokerages. An interesting thing about telecom, however, is that although many of the telecom companies are now selling infrastructure for the Internet, many of them are not e-businesses. So, for example, simple things like, can you go to your local phone company's Web site and pay your bill or dispute a charge of your bill and have it resolved electronically—

Colombo: —or change some element of your service?

Lochhead: Right. To this day, your answer is still, "No."

Colombo: Let me ask the question another way, then. There are a lot of things that you can do on the Web, from brochureware to transactions to customer service. Is there a useful way to think of how different capabilities line up with different industries or different business models?

Lochhead: The problem that we had in the old CRM [Customer Relationship Management] days, we now have in spades on the Internet: The customer has more access points to your business from a sales or service point of view. So the real issue is not so much "Is it going to be clicks and mortar?" but instead it's, "How much clicks and how much mortar?" Entire businesses will be different than they were. Take buying a car. Most customers do not want to buy a car from a "lie until they buy" salesperson. So they'll do their research on the Internet and many people are starting to buy cars on the Internet. Other people still want to take a test drive. But even if they don't test drive it, they still need to get it serviced, right? And you still can't get an oil change on the Internet. Clearly, the sales channel in that business is changing because you and I do our research, we do our comparisons, we know the dealer invoice, we do all that stuff at a minimum, even if we actually physically do the transaction at the dealership. So, maybe the dealer is no longer the principle sales agent but a service agent. The sales/service mix of an industry changes depending on how much clicks and how much mortar it looks like it's going to need to have. But it doesn't mean that salespeople necessarily go away. It just means that the mix of sales and service might change and the role of the salespeople might change. So in a given business, you might actually get more service people and fewer salespeople over time.

Colombo: For a retailer to start to put e-business capabilities together in a way that enhances what they're doing in stores, then, what are some of the things they need to be thinking about?

Lochhead: Let me give you a concrete example about a high-end cosmetics retailer called Sephora that carries all the top brands. The stores are only in prime retail locations; the flagship is on the Champs Eleysses in Paris. Sephora is the Nike Town of cosmetics. When the company wanted to move to the Internet and build a click-and-mortar business, it wanted it to be completely integrated, to provide a unified customer experience. The reason is that the company's competitive advantage is a customer experience—in which consumers browse stores set up by category (for example, perfume or lipstick) and where salespeople only assist if asked. It's a very open environment that the company wanted to bring to the Internet. It wanted *Sephora.com* to offer an electronic experience that, on one hand, mimicked the experience in the store but, on the other hand, leveraged some of the things that you can get on the Internet—the convenience, vast amounts of information right there for browsing, electronic gift certificates, and electronic newsletters. The impact of the fact that you couldn't actually try on an eye shadow is minimized. And the company wanted to be completely integrated with their existing business.

The other thing Sephora did was hook its site into kiosks. If you're in Vegas and make a purchase, but you don't want to carry your merchandise home in your luggage, you can have it shipped to your home right off the kiosk. So the physical location has the kiosks in it, plus the Internet, and it all hangs together at the back end. And that's a much more compelling model than just a brick-and-mortar model, and it's a much more compelling model than just an electronic model.

Colombo: So the experience on the Web has to mirror in some way what a company is trying to achieve in its stores?

Lochhead: Retailers would want to create an experience that imitates their stores, because you want customers to have an equally high set of experiences and you want to have integrity in that brand experience across all touch points—whether it's a call center, a sales rep, a distributor, a retail location, the Internet, or a Palm Pilot.

Colombo: There are companies where, if you buy something from their Web site, you can't return it at their stores. Is that smart?

Lochhead: It's basically one of the stupidest things you could possibly do. You have one customer, and that customer has one experience with you. They don't have a Web experience, a call center experience, and a physical experience. You are one brand to that customer. The other thing too, frankly, is: Why wouldn't I be able to order groceries off the Internet, you have them waiting for me at the store, and I pick them up?

Colombo: Exactly! Well, that's another area of low-hanging fruit. There are few companies that are starting to do that. Circuit City comes to mind. I can go on the Web site and look for a minidisk recorder or something. The site says I can buy it on the Web site and they'll ship it and it'll take so long to reach me. Or, it says, there are three stores within 25 miles of my zip code. The store in downtown Orlando doesn't have it in stock right now, but the store in Altamonte Springs has three, etc.

Lochhead: Do you want to pick it up, do you want us to ship it to you, what do you want to do?

Colombo: The point is that if you want to pick it up, you don't even have to go to or call the store to see if it's in stock—they're doing that step for you on-line. You can look right here and see that it's in stock at this particular store, which makes loads of sense to me.

What are some of the other things that you see companies doing?

Lochhead: Single log-on is a big issue in big companies. What does that mean? Well, nobody at Chase owns George Colombo.

Colombo: Right, because there's the mortgage department and...

Lochhead: ...and the credit card department, and the loan department. Say you want to go to the site and pay your credit card bill, transfer money out of your savings account, and buy a mutual fund. On many companies' sites—and not just in financial services—you have to go to six different sites and re-log in, and one site doesn't know what the other is doing. And so one thing Chase did that doesn't sound like a breakthrough, but it surely is a breakthrough for a company of that magnitude, is a single sign-on. You go online, you sign onto one site, and every component of the bank that you do business with, you can do from one interface. For a company that has millions of customers, the ability to actually aggregate and integrate around the customer with single sign-on and be able to do all that stuff is a huge thing.

Colombo: Absolutely. And the irony of that example is if I am one of your better customers, which is to say I'm doing more things with you, I am more disadvantaged that if I only do one type of business with you. It's as though the company is saying, "If you're going to do a lot of business with us, we'll *really* abuse you!" Let's go back to this point about coordinating brick and mortar with the Web. Does it make sense to be bi-directional? To allow a salesperson to somehow identify me in a system and say, "Oh, Mr. Colombo, you have this drill that you bought on our Web site and these are the things that you would need with it or this is a replacement part or..."

Lochhead: Yes, but it will probably be two to five years before that's a reality. It will probably look like a credit card that you and I carry. It may slip into a Palm-type device that you pull out and you hand to the guy and it gives him your home address, what your inventory of stuff is, all that because you have a "smart home." That sounds really Star Trek, but it's not that far out if you look at emerging technologies. You'll go to buy some paint and the salesperson will say, "Nah, that yellow won't work with the color of your carpet." That's absolutely coming.

Colombo: That's technically feasible, but will it be culturally feasible? Will people be willing to have the salesperson see everything they've bought online?

Lochhead: Everybody is funny about this privacy issue. The real issue is what companies do with the data. Do they mine it anonymously? Do they sell it? What's their policy on how they use it? If they use it as a way to build intimacy with the customer that drives customer advocacy, that creates emotional switching costs, that is a potent competitive weapon and is something that dramatically increases the customers' enjoyment of using or experiencing your brand, that's fine. If they use it in a 1984 Big Brother way, if they sell it to other people, and so on, then those companies are going to get crushed.

Colombo: You use a phrase that I think is interesting: "the cost of switching." What can companies do across the touch points to a customer—whether it's on the Web or in the stores—to build a relationship that starts to raise the pain of switching, that marries the customer to the company?

Lochhead: In a recent study we conducted, we discovered that price is *not* a big motivator for people. Convenience, although it's important in some demographics, is not as important. The most important thing with buying on the Internet is entertainment. In other words, how much fun is this?

Colombo: Is that true across the business-to-customer segment?

Lochhead: This is business-to-customer e-tailing. But we believe it's the same for business-to-business. And we've developed a process on how to cut a deal. First, you have to arouse the customer. Next, they evaluate you, they evaluate your site, and ultimately they evaluate your product or service, which constitutes buying it. For the most part on the Internet, people have been focused on arousing and attracting customers and converting them to transactions. But just because you got somebody to process a transaction doesn't mean you have a customer. So, how do you go from them buying to them becoming an advocate for you?

Colombo: How do you "capture" the customer?

Lochhead: That's right. And advocacy is when loyalty starts to live, right? Once they get to advocacy and they're regularly using the product, that's when they move to what we call an emotional switching cost.

Colombo: So how do you get them to advocacy?

Lochhead: First of all, the product or service offering itself has to be great. Then the next thing is, what's the experience of doing business with you on the Internet? Is that experience repeatable, is it consistent across all touch points: call center, salesperson, physical location, Palm VII, the Internet, kiosks? There's also the whole community and communal aspect of it. Does your customer feel that he or she belongs to something, is part of something? Does he feel as though he can share information with other enthusiasts about this product or service? There's got to be something around the relationship. Otherwise your product is just a commodity.

Colombo: So a business model that's based on just one thing is going to be less and less viable—Amazon is capturing customers with books and then, you may as well drop a CD in the basket and you may as well drop your MP3 player and we'll just ship it all together.

Lochhead: Yes. On top of broadening the offering, there's also the whole notion of when you create an emotional switching cost. You want to get your company to the point where your customer identifies with it and your brand experience is part of a regularity in his or her life. And once that happens, you actually become embedded in your customer's life. The reason Yahoo is what Yahoo is has to do with the fact that it's actually embedded in the way its customers live daily now.

Colombo: Right, because my calendar's there and all those kinds of things; I just can't give those up.

Lochhead: Right.

Colombo: So, as a businessperson it's incumbent upon me to think of what things I could be delivering to my customers to keep that cost of switching as high as possible.

Lochhead: Yes, and the thing of the switching costs that was a breakthrough for us is that a lot of companies try to create a transactionally oriented switching cost. In other words, if you switch from MCI to AT&T, we'll give you this discount. But how do you create an *emotional* switching cost? Yahoo comes up with "My Yahoo." I invest the 15 minutes to set that up. I go there, I now have an attachment to it. My data's there, my information's there, it's part of my life, and now I have an affinity towards the brand. There are no negative costs. The emotional costs are much more compelling.

An Unstoppable Arsenal of Winning Strategies and Tactics

Chapter 5

Don't Just Sell. Capture Customers!

Aperennial line that you hear from motivational speakers at sales meetings goes something like this: "If you always do what you've always done, you'll always get the results that you've always gotten." Oh, for the good old days! The fact of the matter is that, in today's hyper-competitive business environment, if you always do what you've always done, you'll fall further and further behind your competitors, who are consistently raising the competitive bar to new heights.

We've already discussed most of the implications of hyper-competition, so I'm not going to belabor them here. What I do want to point out, however, is the fact that hyper-competition is occurring in conjunction with a few other characteristics of the marketplace that you already know about.

For one thing, the cost of acquiring a new customer is greater than it has ever been before. The proliferation of competitors, the proliferation of marketing media, and the skepticism of the marketplace are combining to make it extraordinarily expensive to add every new addition to you customer list.

In fact, in many industries today, the cost of acquiring a new customer exceeds the average margin that's made in the initial sale to that customer. In other words, businesses regularly lose money on their first sale to a particular customer. In the direct marketing industry, an industry in which this approach is commonplace, this is known as "going negative."

What sense does that make? After all, as I've noted before, you can't lose money on each customer and make it up in volume. The answer lies in the calculation that these businesses make of the lifetime value of each customer. They calculate the percentage of customers that is likely to return to do additional business over time, and they calculate the average volume of that additional business along with its margin contribution. The resulting figure represents the lifetime value of each new customer. For years, businesses in industries such as direct marketing have understood that it makes perfect sense to make little or no money on an initial sale to a new customer (or even to go slightly negative) in order to add that customer to the active customer roster.

Although this may represent new and apparently risky thinking to businesses that are not familiar with this model, in a hyper-competitive business environment, this sort of approach is destined to become the rule, not the exception. In fact, when you combine the increased cost of customer acquisition with the depressed profit margins that hyper-competition is imposing on many industries, the prospect of making an initial sale with little or no profit is almost not optional. The only thing that's optional is whether or not you build a sales and marketing structure that allows you to systematically exploit every customer's lifetime value.

The Two "Ends" of Your Relationship With Your Customers

The best place to begin building that kind of structure is to start thinking of your dealings with your customers in terms of a front end and a back end. The front end represents everything that you do to acquire the customer, up to and including the initial purchase the customer makes from your company. The back end is everything that happens after that initial purchase.

Most businesses are relentlessly focused on the front end. Of course, there's nothing wrong with paying lots of attention to the front end. After all, every year you're going to lose some of your existing customers for one reason or another. Some will move, some will go out of business, some will die, and some will start buying from their brother-in-law who just got in the business. For all of these reasons and more, you're going to lose customers all the time for reasons that are beyond your control, so you'll want to make sure you're replacing the customers you lose. In addition, adding new customers represents one of the three fundamental approaches to growing your business. It makes perfect sense to be systematically adding new customers all the time.

But assuming that your business is not in startup mode, it's a great deal easier and considerably more profitable to cultivate your past and present customers. A dollar invested in marketing to your customer base will almost always yield far greater returns than that same dollar will if it's invested in the pursuit of new customers. That's true for several reasons:

@   **Reaching existing customers is less expensive.** You've already made the investment in acquiring these customers, so you don't need to use expensive media to reach them. You can reach them relatively inexpensively from now on.

@   **Existing customers are more responsive.** Your existing customers are already familiar with who you are. They're much less skeptical than prospects who haven't yet learned about you.

@   **Back end products are often more profitable.** If you sell appliances, for example, your back end product might be a service contract or supplies. Either will typically have much better margins than you were able to get on the initial sale.

By the way, just because you're marketing to existing customers doesn't mean that you're foregoing meaningful growth. I mentioned that acquiring new customers is one of the three fundamental approaches to growing your business. The other two approaches are selling more of your existing products to existing customers and selling additional products to existing customers. Both of these two growth strategies (particularly the second one) are basically back end strategies.

Now, all of this is irrefutable. New customers are difficult to sell to and expensive to acquire. Existing customers are easier to sell to and much more profitable. Here's the amazing thing: Most businesses have no serious back end strategy. This is a strategic failing that you can't afford. If you're going to survive and succeed in today's business environment, then you're going to need a strategy and a structure that will allow you to easily, inexpensively, and effectively market and sell to your existing customers.

Where All Great Back End Efforts Begin

Let me start out with a point that might seem obvious but that is absolutely critical to how you can proceed from here:

The whole concept of a back end strategy falls apart if you don't have a way to contact your existing customers. This seems as though it is the most straightforward concept in the world, but before we move forward, I want you to consider a couple of things. First, think about the last few times you did business with someone for the first time. Apart from situations where it was required by the nature of the transaction, how many times were you asked for your name or address? My guess is darned few. The experience I had at a local executive golf course is likely to be more typical. After my round, I asked the guy behind the counter in the pro shop if the course offered any kind of membership or frequent player arrangement. It didn't, I was told, but the owners were thinking about offering one. I asked how I'd be able to find out if that happened. The answer was that I'd just have to keep my eyes open whenever I stopped in.

"Don't you maintain a mailing list of customers?" I asked.

"Nope," was the predictable, almost inevitable, reply.

The other thing you should think about is how seldom you're contacted even by those businesses that bother to get your contact information. Classic examples of this kind of neglect are the dozens and dozens of restaurants I've been to with a fishbowl or open briefcase waiting at the checkout counter. "Drop Your Business Card In Here For a Chance to Win a Free Lunch!" says the sign. I drop my business card in every single time. (What can I tell you? I'm an optimist.) Not only have I never won the free lunch (which is bad enough), but I have never—not once—been contacted by any of these restaurants with any kind of follow-up marketing offer. Not being bright enough to capture customer information in the first place is one thing, but capturing it and then never using it is absolutely incredible.

This kind of neglect is not going to help you achieve your sales and marketing objectives. You need to develop a system that captures the information you need to market effectively to your existing customers. In fact, I'm going to encourage you to take this concept to the next level and not only collect contact information, but also to collect as much additional information as possible. (In Chapter 13, we'll discuss ways to do this along with strategies for dealing with the privacy issues that will inevitably arise.)

At a minimum, here is the information that you want to collect:

@ Name.

@ Address.

@ Phone number.

@ E-mail address.

How do you get this information? Well, if you begin your customer relationship by transacting business online, you're at an advantage because it's all built in to the process. It's information you need in order to fulfill an order. Some "offline" business relationships also require most of this information. For example, it's impossible to write an insurance policy without getting most of this information. The possible exception is the client's e-mail address, but, once you're in an information gathering mode, it's simple to build that additional question into the process.

The challenge is in those other instances where the situation doesn't inherently require that you collect the information. This is usually the case in a retail situation, for example. The most straightforward approach to getting the information you need in those situations is to ask for it. It's remarkable how easy it is if you just build a few questions into your selling process. No retailer I can think of does this better than Radio Shack. If you go into a Radio Shack store to just buy a couple of AA batteries, the first question you get at the cash register is, "May I please have your phone number?" From there, the system checks to see if you're already on file.

If not, the salesperson matter-of-factly asks you for your contact information before the transaction proceeds.

Contact information is a good place to start, but it is hardly the only kind of information you want to collect. If possible, your information systems should be designed in a way that allows you to accumulate a history of your customer's purchases. This kind of information can be extremely valuable as you move your customers up the relationship hierarchy I described in Chapter 1 and that value extends beyond marketing offers.

Consider the case of an electronics retailer. A particular customer bought a wide screen television several years ago and has been enjoying the television, as well as an ongoing relationship with the retailer, ever since. Now the customer is ready to purchase a DVD player. Access to the customer's purchasing history means that the sales associate won't have to guess at what kind of inputs the customer's television has. As a result, the sales associate can make the right recommendation for cabling and the customer can leave the store confident that the DVD player is going to install painlessly.

Use Information Effectively

Deploying any of these approaches depends on your company's ability to use information effectively. There are two factors that will determine how successful you are at doing this.

Information is available where it's needed in real time.

Everyone in your organization who has contact with a customer needs access to information about that customer. Also, your customers need to be able to access their information via the Web. From a management standpoint, your job is to anticipate what information is likely to be needed and then to make sure that it's available. In general, too much information is better than too little. Making information available in "real time" is also important. Delta Airlines is one example of a company that's good at this. If I fly from my home in the Orlando area to Atlanta, I can check my Sky Miles account from a Crown Room in Atlanta and it will already reflect the flight that I just deplaned. *That* is real time. The payoff is the tremendous amount of confidence it creates on the part of customers.

Your information systems talk to each other.

As I've said elsewhere in this book (and will no doubt repeat a few more times before I'm through), customers don't care about your company's internal systems issues. They want information and they want results. They want the confidence that results from their Web interactions with your company and their in-person interactions being integrated smoothly, seamlessly, and transparently.

Here's some food for thought. When you're thinking about deploying information effectively, you should ask yourself these questions:

@   How can I use information to make my customer feel more confident?

@   What information is my customer likely to want?

@   From where is he or she likely to want to access it?

@   How is he or she likely to want to get it?

@   What information will my employees need to serve customers more effectively?

@   How can I use information to anticipate my customers' needs and wants?

@   Is there a way to deploy information that will just blow my customers' socks off?

Once again, *Amazon.com* provides an instructive example of coming up with creative answers to a few of these questions. Let me share a story that illustrates what I'm talking about.

Many years ago, I came across a book titled *Influence* by a brilliant psychologist named Robert Cialdini. It was a sensational book. It absolutely floored me, so much so that I contacted Dr. Cialdini through his office at Arizona State University and made arrangements with him to use material from his book as the foundation of some sales training workshops that my company was offering at the time.

Fast forward several years. The Internet had exploded and, as a perennial early adopter, I was not only a regular surfer, but I had also begun buying books from Amazon. I had been a regular customer of Amazon's for well more than a year before I ever got the urge to take a look at their recommendations for me. (Amazon monitors your purchases over time and, based on those purchases, compiles a list of books that were bought by people who bought books that you've bought.) When I finally clicked on the link to see which books Amazon recommended for me, I'll bet you can guess what was waiting there for me. Of course! *Influence* by Robert Cialdini. That's a great example of using information to anticipate a customer's likely needs and wants. (It's also not a bad example of deploying information in a way that blows a customer's socks off!)

Make Customer Satisfaction a Priority

Building a substantial and reliable back end business is not just a matter of making marketing contact with existing customers on a regular basis, though (although obviously it's an indispensable part of the process of capturing customers). Your success with your back end will depend on your ability to cultivate your relationship with your customers. And technology is not the only factor that will determine your success in these efforts, although companies that can use technology skillfully will always be at an advantage over those that don't. Success at cultivating customer relationships is a result of making it a conscious priority.

One approach to customer satisfaction that is starting to make headway among forward-thinking companies is the appointment of a chief customer officer (CCO), a senior corporate executive whose portfolio is simply to make certain that customers are happy, someone who is focused on maintaining the quality of the relationship that a company has with its customers. Ginger Kernachan, a longtime analyst in the sales force automation/customer relationship management industry, was one of the first journalists anywhere to describe this nascent position in a provocative piece she wrote for *CRM Magazine*. According to Ginger, the existence of this position is a tangible indication of a company's commitment to customer satisfaction. In addition, she cites the work of research analysts in the e-business arena who estimate that by the year 2003, fully 25 percent of the largest companies in the world will have established such a position.

Whether the CCO position establishes itself as a mainstream approach or not, the thinking behind the creation of the position is what's important. Customer satisfaction is not just a benchmark of performance. It is an explicit marketing strategy for companies that understand the value of a healthy back end. Technology will enable your efforts, but it won't happen without a conscious effort to get it done.

Now that we've established a foundation for coordinating your "real world" sales and marketing efforts with the presence your company is establishing on the Web, it's time to start examining some specific strategies for making that happen. That's exactly what we're going to do in Chapter 6, and we're going to start by examining principles for creating a congruent presence in the marketplace.

Create a Congruent Presence in the Marketplace

If you're looking for new ways to alienate customers, the Internet offers some great opportunities. There are a number of creative ways to do this, but here's my personal favorite: Design a business structure that separates your Web customers from the rest of your business. And if a Web customer shows up at one of your regular business outlets with a question, problem, or complaint, then turn him away and send him home to his computer to try to resolve the issue. You don't think that anyone could be that dumb? Au contraire!

A major bank launched an online banking division a few years ago. Although the new division was given its own brand name and identity, its relationship with the parent was not-so-subtlety leveraged in order to give it the kind of credibility and security that a pure

Internet startup would lack. That wasn't a bad idea. In fact, it was a perfectly plausible strategy in an industry where safety and reliability are so important to customers. Problems arose, though, when the company's online customers started turning up at the parent bank's branches with questions about their accounts or other problems. These customers couldn't get the time of day from anyone working in the branches. The Web customers were brushed off and told that they needed to go back online if they wanted to get help. You won't be surprised to hear that many of these customers decided that the only online help they wanted was help in canceling their accounts. The CEO who designed this ill-conceived strategy is now gone. With any kind of luck, his successor will have a better appreciation for the need to coordinate online and offline efforts.

Flunking Customer Satisfaction 101

The sad truth is that among those companies that do business both online and off, it is the rule rather than the exception to see the kind of problem I just described. This finding was echoed recently by a study done by The Gartner Group. According to a report on that study which appeared in *The Daily eStat*, on online publication of *eMarketer.com*, 50 of the leading e-retail sites on the Web were assessed to determine the quality of their Customer Relationship Management (CRM) efforts. None of the sites was rated "Excellent" or even "Good." Less than a quarter of the sites were considered "Average."

The *eMarketer.com* report of the study went on to say:

> *Of the sites surveyed, half were pure-plays and half were click-and-mortar. The pure-plays were more adept at CRM than the traditionally based retailers.*

Most retail call centers treat Internet customers like strangers. Marketers are not integrating their Web sites and call centers and when disappointed customers call, the representatives are blind to their Web activities and transactions.

Some of the underlying cause for this unfortunate and counterproductive situation is understandable, if not excusable. In every instance that I have reviewed, companies that are doing business both online and offline are brick-and-mortar companies that have ventured on to the Web. There are no instances that I've been able to find (yet) of a major dotcom company venturing out into the world of bricks and mortar. This trend, then, is not some sort of unspoken animosity towards Web customers. In fact, these companies are investing heavily to attract customers on the Web. Instead, what's going on is that these companies are gravitating towards the mode of business that they're most familiar with, towards the mode of business that their systems were designed to deal with. In any event, the clear tendency is for companies that have both online and offline customers to treat the online customers as second class citizens.

What's the Problem?

Part of the problem with many companies is a kind of Internet parochialism that existed among many Internet cognoscenti. In their minds, the world of bricks and mortar was obsolete, inefficient, and—the most damning thing of all—*uncool.* They believed (or, at least, they told anyone who would listen) that commerce in the future was going to be almost entirely electronic. They believed that stores and branch offices would be relegated to the dustbins of history. As you know, a funny thing happened on the way to an all-digital future.

Another problem is the result of the fact that, for a long time, the stock market was distorting everyone's view of reality, causing businesses to commit unnatural acts in order to take advantage of the dotcom exuberance (that is, hysteria) that permeated the market. You've heard all of the stories. The marketplace was rewarding dotcom startups that had never earned a dime with market capitalizations that far exceed those placed on brick-and-mortar competitors that had demonstrable track records of profitability. Even if brick-and-mortar companies were making demonstrable online efforts, the market seemed to ignore them. "Only pure dotcom players need apply," it seemed to be saying.

Artificial Separation

Well, the managers in charge of these companies got the message. As a result, the online bank that I previously described was created, along with a host of other dotcom spinoffs of brick-and-mortar companies. These businesses were completely separate from their parent companies. If the markets wanted dotcom, then they were going to get dotcom. The upshot of all of this was that the business structures of these dotcom spinoffs were not designed to respond to the needs of customers or to address the operational needs of the companies that created them. They were designed to take advantage of equity markets that were throwing unimaginable amounts of money at anything that looked like a dotcom business.

What's obvious now, though, is that this approach might have made sense to the stock market (although that's clearly not as true as it used to be), but it didn't make any sense from an operational standpoint. And it made no sense at all from the standpoint of addressing customers' needs. Even if these companies didn't completely alienate their customers, they certainly didn't see the huge long-term opportunity in building a sales and marketing structure that integrates online and offline efforts.

Not everyone made that mistake, though. A few companies understood what the world is certainly going to look like someday and they began to structure their businesses to take advantage of it.

One instructive example is Circuit City (*Circuitcity.com*), a company that is providing a glimpse of some of what the future might look like. At first glance, Circuit City's Web site provides its customers with a shopping experience that isn't too different from any one of dozens of other online electronics retailers. It offers pricing and information on its products along with various special pricing offers. It's when the customer is ready to buy that things start to get really interesting.

The customer is asked to input her zip code. She's then notified of which Circuit City stores are in her immediate area. (If there's more than one, she's allowed to pick the one that's most convenient.) The Web site designates this store as her Express Pickup location. The company's Web site goes on to explain the terms and conditions of using the Express Pickup option:

> *You may choose to complete your purchase online and pick up your product at a local Circuit City store near you using our Express Pickup option.*
>
> *Express Pickup purchases may be completed between 8am to 10pm daily in your local time zone and picked up during regular store hours.*
>
> *By choosing Express Pickup you will pay no shipping charges, in addition, you have the flexibility of picking up your purchase at your convenience. Your purchase is immediately available for pickup after you have received your order confirmation page.*

Express Pickup is our fastest, cheapest and most convenient way for you to get your product.

What Makes It Work

There are three elements of what Circuit City is doing with Express Pickup that are worth your attention.

1. **The customer has the option of picking up his order at a local store.** This is a great starting point for distinguishing Circuit City from every other consumer electronics Web site. All other things being equal, once you've decided to purchase something, wouldn't you rather have it right now? More importantly, it also distinguishes the company from its brick-and-mortar competitors, none of whom (as of this writing) offer this option. The company's Web and store presences don't compete with each other; they provide leverage for each other. The company is agnostic on the issue of how it wants the customer to shop. As a result, the customer gets to shop however he or she prefers at any given time.

2. **The transaction can be completed at the customer's convenience.** As soon as a confirmation page is produced on the Web site, the order is ready for pickup by the customer at the store. There is no need to wait for the transaction to get posted. If the customer wants instant gratification, it's there. If the customer wants to pick up the product on her way home from work, that's fine, too.

3. **The system works in real time.** Here's the most interesting (and instructive) element of how this whole deal works. While the customer is online

shopping, there's a real time look-through to the store's inventory. In other words, while the customer is online—*before* she places her order—she knows whether or not a particular item is in stock at the store of her choice. If it's not, she can check its availability at other nearby Circuit City stores and designate her order for pickup at any store that has the item in stock.

At the risk of beating this to death, let me emphasize the conceptual foundation that this system is built on, because it is the key to success for any of your efforts along these lines. This system doesn't care how the customer wants to do business. It's agnostic. It's designed to accommodate customers' preferences at any given time. If the customer wants to pick up a purchase at the store, that's fine. If the customer wants his purchase delivered, that's okay, too. And if the customer has different preferences at different times for different purchases, that's not a problem, either.

Avoiding a Big Pitfall

The general ideas found in the Circuit City example can be applied to any business model. Some questions arise, though, in terms of implementation. In the business-to-business arena, for example, the most common questions that come up are in the area of compensation. Many managers are reluctant to fully compensate salespeople for sales that take place on the Web. They believe that the salesperson should receive less compensation if a customer places an order on the company's Web site.

Let's assume that a company has organized its sales organization around a structure of assigned accounts or designated territories. In other words, a salesperson has certain specific accounts that are assigned to him or her, or that salesperson is responsible for managing and growing the company's business in a particular geographic location. In either case, it seems to me that a policy of penalizing the salesperson for orders that are placed on the Web is going to be counterproductive for a variety of reasons.

The most important reason is that it violates the principle of designing a structure that is agnostic regarding how the customer chooses to buy. You can try to implement any sort of sales directives that you want, but the simple fact of the matter is that salespeople will always favor those activities for which they get compensated. If salespeople don't get compensated fully for orders that are placed on the Web, it's almost inevitable that they will subtly (or, maybe, not-so-subtly) discourage your customers from ordering online.

Or, to put it differently, your customers will be discouraged from using a more cost-effective, more efficient method of ordering. They will be disadvantaged, and your company will be disadvantaged. It's not your salespeople's fault. In this situation, they're just responding logically to the structure of their compensation scheme. It is irrational to expect them to act in a way that is not in their best interest.

It would be far more rational—and far more effective—to implement a compensation structure that doesn't penalize salespeople whose customers order online. In the end, it is in everyone's interest for them to do this, so what sense would it make to pinch pennies?

In today's hyper-competitive business environment, your strategy should be to move your salespeople up the value chain in terms of their interactions with customers. You don't need them to be taking orders and, in fact, you don't *want* them to be taking orders. You want them to move beyond a tactical, low-level relationship with your customers into more of a strategic, high-level relationship. Instead of taking orders, you want them creating a systematic structural relationship between your company and your customers. Don't fall into the trap of shortsightedness when it comes to compensation. If you've got the right salespeople in place, then let them focus on the important things. Let them move your customers in a direction that's right for the customers and right for your company when it comes to how orders are placed. And don't try to insist they take a hit in their compensation for doing so.

Online/Offline Synergy

If you're doing things right, your online and offline efforts should be designed to complement each other. Bed Bath & Beyond is a retail outlet that has made it a point to communicate to its customers the fact that its stores and Web site (*bedbath.com*) are designed to work together. On its Web site and in much of its marketing materials, it makes the point that anything that's purchased on the Web site can be brought into any one of the company's more than 250 stores for exchange or credit.

Barnes & Noble is an example of a company that has a separate corporate structure for its Web business (*bn.com*), but has put policies in place that make that separation transparent to its customers. In fact, as one of a small group of companies that has as prominent a presence on the Web as it has in bricks and mortar, it is well-positioned to help define what a congruent presence in the marketplace should look like in the future.

One fascinating and critical insight that appears to be developing from Barnes & Noble's experience is that a company's Web business and retail business can thrive simultaneously. In a recent piece in *Fortune*, Barnes & Noble vice chairman Steve Riggio revealed that, contrary to expectations, his company's Web site does not appear to be cannibalizing shoppers from its stores. Instead, the overall pie is growing as the Web and the stores both work together to reinforce the overall strength of the Barnes & Noble brand.

The important thing to remember is that your customers are your customers, no matter where they came from or how they choose to do business with you. There is a tremendous competitive advantage waiting for you in the marketplace if you have the vision and can exert the discipline to establish a unified, congruent presence in the marketplace.

Once you've started to unify your company's online and offline efforts, you're ready to move on to the next step in capturing customers: targeted customer communication, electronic and otherwise, which is the topic of Chapter 7.

Bob Lewis

Bob Lewis is a columnist for InfoWorld, one of the IT industry's most important trade journals. He is also the co-author, with his father, Herschell Gordon Lewis, of Selling on the Net, *one of the first significant books on the market about e-commerce.*

Colombo: What advantages does a small business have on the Web?

Lewis: What we need to understand about information technology is that, for the most part, there are diseconomies of scale. This means that small businesses, if they have aggressive instincts and the willingness to invest in the business, actually have some advantages over larger businesses.

For example, inexpensive servers are the hallmark of the Internet. If you operate a small business, you can thrive in that environment forever. What's even better is that you can run inexpensive packaged software. A small businessperson can wrap his or her business around these low-cost alternatives and be just as happy as can be. And he'll have a business and technical environment that is still small enough to be manageable.

Giant corporations have huge scalability problems and huge manageability problems, and they have all of the distressing realities of global commerce, including the expense and the logistics of maintaining multilingual, multicultural, multicurrency sites. Chances are, a small to medium-sized business is selling primarily in the United States. It's far easier to manage your advertising and promotional copy so that it sells in both Mississippi and California than it is to manage copy that will sell simultaneously in Korea, Sweden, Germany, and the U.K.

Colombo: What are some of the things that a small business can do on its Web site that are interesting and effective but not prohibitively expensive?

Lewis: There are a variety of tools—such as shopping cart capabilities—that are relatively easy to build into a site now. On the other hand, large corporations must have full integration of their Web systems with their complicated back end systems. So if you're selling toys during the Christmas season, your online customers expect to see whether the toy's in stock, because their kids expect them to know. For a large corporation, real time inventory tracking is a big and complicated issue. For a small company, if you can't afford the technology, you can have an employee update a static Web page periodically during the peak season and get away with it. It's certainly not optimal, but the point is that you can do it.

Also, large companies have to work with high-margin, large integrators just to get the talent, experience, and resident expertise that they need to create a fully integrated Web site. For the small to medium-sized business, there are huge numbers of very hungry, small developers and integrators that would just love to do your Web site for you, which means that you don't need to maintain the technical talent in-house. You can farm it out at very attractive rates.

Colombo: That makes sense. It also seems as though large companies have a tendency to want to build the flashiest, latest, and greatest Web sites with all the newest plug-ins. But not only is it expensive, it's disadvantageous in the market-place.

Lewis: Absolutely. Everything about the Web is the same as everything about every other medium, which is to say "know thy client, know thy customer" and match your selling tech-nique to his or her interests. There are some environments where flashy is important. If you're *Wired* magazine on the Web, for example, a dry text site is going to be at variance with your corporate image, and you will lose credibility. If, on the other hand, you are an automotive parts manufacturer and what you're trying to do is sell add-on parts to the automotive hob-byist market, the chances are very good that you don't need rock music coming out of your site while you have a Volkswagen dancing on the screen, because the people who are on your site don't want that. They want that strange thing that makes the front of their Beetle look like a Mercedes.

Colombo: And they want it quickly.

Lewis: Right. The keys are fulfillment and speed of down-load. The only fancy things that you'll usually need on your site are actual photographs of what your customer is buying. The important thing here is that you want them to download quickly. There is that perennial balance between how much you put on one page and how long it takes the page to load. Although there's no perfect solution, it's important to always anticipate the low-est common denominator for your customers' technology and build to that. And do more than build to it-test to it as well.

Colombo: In other words, you need to be mindful of the tech-nical environment that your customer is likely to be working in.

Lewis: Exactly, and be mindful of the mindset he'll be in when he's visiting your Web site. The purchasing manager of a car dealership's service department at the office is going to want a very prosaic site where he can order the parts he needs as fast as he can order them. The same person at home working with his child on a homework assignment may want an encyclopedia site with all the flashy multimedia he can get. He's the same person but in a different role. And in that role, he has an entirely different mindset.

Colombo: Right, and different expectations.

Lewis: Exactly.

Colombo: What is the biggest misconception that small businesses have about building an effective Web presence?

Lewis: "We have to be an e-commerce site this year or we'll die!" It's like everything else in the known universe: The generalities are cool, but if you make a business decision based on what you've read the trend is, you're doomed before you start, because you're adopting somebody else's solution and just hoping that you're like everybody else. If, in fact, you sell in an environment where personal relationships matter, then it's perfectly fine to have just an online brochure and an 800 number. If you want to be really fancy—because I do believe in letting people order the moment they make a decision—have a simple order form online that a human being on the other end processes. You don't need the ultimate in technological sophistication to succeed on the Web. You need to anticipate and deliver your customers' requirements.

Colombo: It's almost heresy, but there are some businesses for which brochureware is just fine.

Lewis: Absolutely. I saw an analysis recently that scored a couple of dozen Web sites. One of the criteria was whether they were personalized. Every site that wasn't personalized was marked down in the assessment, which of course means that the person doing the grading is making the fatuous assumption that every business must always personalize in order to succeed. Personalization on the Web is a fine thing to do for some companies or some customer groups. In other cases, personalization is not the answer because that's not the business model.

The fact is, this whole concept of personalization is misdirected in some cases. The idea of personalization is that your company treats each customer as an individual. That's a great idea, but it doesn't mean customers will create a personal relationship with your Web site. It's not going to work that way. It is quite true that people can form personal relationships with companies. If you don't believe that, go to Wrigley Field [in Chicago] and you'll find that the ballpark is packed full of raving fans who don't care that their team is a losing team. For the Cubs, losing is part of their mystique. But that's a real team of real human beings.

The fact that a Web site can deliver a personalized message doesn't mean that there's any real emotional connection going on. So if you focus on using personalization technology on your Web site, you will never provide a facility for creating any emotional connection. All you'll create is sterile benefit. If, on the other hand, part of your personalization technique on the Web is to open a chat window in the middle of a visitor's session and have a real live human being start interacting with the visitor—and then give that real live human being access to every bit of information you have about that visitor—now you create the facility for emotional connection between your customer and your company, which is exactly what you want to do if you want to maximize the revenue that you derive from every visitor to your Web site. And if you constantly focus on success in person-to-person interactions, which I call P2P, then your business maximizes its chance for success. Small to medium-sized businesses, because of the diseconomies of scale on the Web, may have the best opportunity to exploit P2P.

Colombo: What you're saying is that it's important to avoid being lemming-like, doing whatever is in all the Web magazines. You don't want to approach the Web saying, "This month the latest thing is X. We have to do it on our site."

Lewis: The hazard and the blessing of being in any business is doing what makes sense for your particular business as opposed to reading about a trend and automatically panicking because you're not following it. There is no one-size-fits-all business strategy.

But there are three strategic advantages that small and medium-sized businesses have over large companies. First, small to medium-sized businesses can move much more quickly than larger corporations. They can make decisions faster, because fewer people need to be involved in them. Second, small and medium-sized companies benefit from diseconomies of scale, which we talked about earlier. Third is a concept actually borrowed from high school biology textbooks, which is the ratio of surface area to volume. What I mean is that the smaller the company, the larger the percentage of employees who care about real, paying customers. Small companies don't have time to worry about nonsensical ideas like "internal customers." In a small company everybody is focused on real, paying customers. In a large company you end up with strange ideas like, "I get paid to make another employee happy." It's a nice thought to make other employees happy, but when you have employees who don't think that their job is to create value for real, paying customers, chances are they won't create value for those customers except by accident.

Colombo: Also, in large companies, you have employees who haven't seen real, paying customers since they've been working there.

Lewis: In large corporations, it's not at all uncommon to find that nine out of 10 employees are focused on making somebody else inside the company happy, and that sales reps are usually viewed as a colossal pain in the neck because they come in with unreasonable demands that don't fit the company policy manual just because some customer wants it.

Colombo: Another important point about the advantages for small to medium-sized companies on the Web is that if you're a business owner or manager who is not technically inclined and feel like you have a blind spot because you don't understand technology, you want to avoid buying into the assumption that just because you don't understand it, it's some kind of special, rarefied atmosphere where basic business principles don't apply.

Lewis: Absolutely.

Colombo: Because they still do.

Lewis: In fact, the Web is not about technology. Technology on the Web itself is extraordinarily simple. If you can handle a modern word processor, you can create a basic Web site. The authoring tools for basic Web sites—by that I mean brochureware sites—are no harder to learn than a sophisticated word processing program. The complexity of technology on the Web is the same as the technology complexity in call centers, which is integration with all of your back end systems and the reconstruction of your business processes. That's where the complexity lies. That's where you need the systems integrators or your internal IT staff. And that's unchanged from the days prior to the Web.

Colombo: So it's the business issues, not the technical issues, that will ultimately win the day.

Lewis: I'll give you that, but here's the tricky part: It's absolutely true that technology without a business purpose is just a bad idea. You always have to know why you're doing something. It's equally true, though—and this is where a company can get into lots of trouble—that by believing that business has to drive the technology, you can miss the fact that it's always technology that creates the new opportunities. So, if you're running a small or medium-sized business, the thing to understand about technology is that technology won't win by itself, but new technology can certainly cause you to lose if you don't keep up with the business capabilities that your competitors create by using it.

Chapter 7

Targeted Communication with Your Customers

In Chapter 5, we looked at the importance of acquiring the kind of information that will allow you to actively communicate with your customers. In this chapter, we're going to look at some guidelines that will allow you to conduct that communication efficiently, effectively, and with a minimum of damage.

"Damage?" you ask incredulously. "What's this about damage?" When it comes to electronic communication, the unfortunate truth is that it's a lot easier than you might think to alienate your customers. And, as many unsuspecting businesses have found out after it's too late, it's not all that difficult to engender outright hostility. From a sales and marketing standpoint, hostility is usually pretty low on the list of reactions that you're looking for!

As it turns out, the perfect medium for efficient and effective customer communications is, unfortunately, the very same one that carries with it a constant potential danger of angering and/or alienating your customers. That medium, of course, is electronic mail. If you're going to do it properly, it's critically important that you understand where the dangers of e-mail marketing lie so that you can avoid them while still taking advantage of the medium's unrivaled potential.

The Rules

When it comes to e-mail marketing, there are two rules that you must always keep in mind. There's nothing that you can learn on this subject—here or anywhere else—that is more important than these two rules, so commit them to memory and review them often:

@   **Rule #1:** Never, ever spam.

@   **Rule #2:** Never, ever forget Rule #1.

Spam is unsolicited commercial e-mail. As a verb, it means to send out large amounts of unsolicited e-mail to recipients who are not familiar with you, have not done business with you in the past, or have not otherwise indicated to you that they would welcome a commercial communication. On the surface, there would seem to be a great deal of justification for doing this. After all, the cost of e-mail is, effectively, nothing. And the cost of acquiring literally millions of e-mail addresses is often just a few dollars. So why wouldn't it make sense? Just a single order or two could cost justify hundreds of thousands of e-mails.

The answer to that question reflects the cultural sensibilities that have evolved on the Internet in its relatively short existence. Simply put, in the world of e-mail, spam is the equivalent of a drive-by shooting. Its apparent economic justification notwithstanding, it has absolutely no place in your arsenal of marketing tools. At least not if your business plan extends beyond the middle of next week.

There are all kinds of theories about why a marketing behavior that is so well-tolerated in one medium (regular mail) is so reviled when it's attempted in a medium that is somewhat different but essentially similar. The bottom line is that this rule is so pervasive, is so well-established, and has been demonstrated to be true for so long, that I'm basically just going to offer it to you at face value.

Your punishment for violating this rule will be swift and certain. In the minds of your target market, you'll be relegated to a place that would make the boiler room in *Glengary Glen Ross* seem like the epitome of a first class sales and marketing organization! And you can be certain that your infamy will quickly spread far beyond the prospects who were the recipients of the offending piece of mail. *Amazon.com* chief Jeff Bezos, in a virtual presentation he gave at the Harvard Business School's *Cyberposium* event, made the observation that word of mouth is far more powerful on the Internet than it is in the "real" world. This dynamic can work in your favor if you're doing things right, but if you acquire a reputation as a spammer, you'll find it difficult, if not altogether impossible, to live down.

If you're intent on sending unsolicited marketing communications to potential customers, then bite the bullet, spend the extra money, and communicate with them through traditional direct-mail campaigns. A marketing message that would raise the wrath of your market if it was delivered via e-mail won't raise an eyebrow if you send it via snail mail.

By the way, just because you're trying to craft a marketing campaign that's suitable for today's "wired" world—even if you're trying to target a techno-savvy group of prospects—don't make the mistake of underestimating direct mail. As we saw in Chapter 3, even pure dotcom companies are making regular use of traditional media to get their message across. Direct mail is definitely one of the media that they're using.

Once a prospect has responded to your direct-mail campaign (or any of your other marketing campaigns, for that matter) though, and has supplied you with his or her e-mail address, then your e-mail contacts with that prospect—as long as you stay within reasonable boundaries—are no longer classifiable as spam.

The Advantages of E-mail

Once you've gotten beyond the issue of spam, there are some things that make e-mail marketing extremely compelling for you as a marketer. It would not overstate the case to say that the ability to engage in e-mail marketing is going to be the end result of most of your online efforts. In fact, in many cases the primary reason for the existence of your Web site in the first place ought to be to act as a vehicle to capture your prospect's e-mail addresses (and other information that will be useful in your marketing efforts). That means that if your site is not capturing this information, it should be considered a failure.

E-mail is a terrific online marketing vehicle for you because:

It's cheap.

As a practical matter, the cost of sending an e-mail message to your customer base (or some subset of your customer base) effectively approaches zero. Printing and delivery costs are no longer part of the calculation. This means that a mailing can be extremely successful, when measured in terms of its return on investment, with a response percentage that is very low.

When you want to get a message out, it's fast.

Any marketing medium will do if your message doesn't need to be timely. But if you want to piggyback your marketing message on something that's in the news, or if there's some kind of time-sensitive market condition that you want to exploit, there isn't anything that even comes close to e-mail. You can create a message and have it sitting in your customers inbox in hours instead of days or weeks.

When you're looking for feedback, it's very fast.

You can test the various elements of a marketing campaign more quickly (by orders of magnitude) than you can in any other medium. You don't have to wait weeks for your feedback. You can have it in days. In fact, you often have much of it within hours.

You can easily "deliver" an interested prospect to a chosen destination.

In most other marketing media, the point at which you ask a prospect to take some kind of action represents a chasm that must be crossed. Depending on the extent of the action, that chasm can be great. For example, there was a time in direct response when a customer had to stop what he or she was doing, clip a coupon, fill it out, write a check, find an envelope, put the check and the coupon in an envelope, put a stamp on the envelope, and then put the envelope in a mailbox. Obviously, with all of those tasks standing between a seller and an order, there was a considerable number of interested prospects who never quite made it to the finish line. The proliferation of credit cards helped bridge the chasm, as did the dawn of toll-free phone numbers. Asking a prospect to remember to make it a point to visit a particular store represents a chasm, too. When a marketing message is sent by e-mail, though, a hyperlink can deliver the prospect instantly to a place where he or she can take action.

Your marketing e-mail can be replicated.

When you're marketing in other media, even if you have the most sensational offer in the world, the chances of a prospect getting actively involved in passing it on to friends and colleagues are slim. Very few prospects are going to make a photocopy of a print ad, for example. And messages that are delivered in media such as radio and television are pretty much confined to the people who happen to hear or see them when they're broadcast. E-mail, on the other hand, tends to be forwarded from one person to another if it's even remotely interesting. As a result, your message can multiply and spread when it's delivered in this medium. (Dell Computer's Small Business Marketing unit sends out e-mail messages to its customers that feature a hyperlink that says, "Click here to forward this e-mail." That's a simple step that no doubt boosts the pass-along factor significantly.)

Doing It Right

Obviously, electronic mail is a marketing medium that is worth using. As I explained earlier in this chapter, not spamming is the single most important rule that you can remember when it comes to e-mail marketing. There are some other factors that will contribute to your success with e-mail:

Have something to say.

If you're like most people, there's someone you know— maybe a co-worker or a relative—who regularly calls you on the phone. For the sake of this discussion, let's call this person Larry. More often than not, Larry manages to reach you when you're in the middle of doing something that requires your undivided attention. Or better yet, Larry calls when you're working under a pressing deadline, hurrying to complete an important project on time. And nine times out of 10, what is

Larry calling to talk about? Nothing. Doesn't it drive you crazy? Doesn't it make you want to reach through the phone cord and give old Larry a smack? Of course it does. You'll do yourself a favor if you remember Larry the next time you're getting ready to send out a marketing message or sales offer by e-mail. Your e-mail is interrupting your prospect. Make sure that, unlike Larry's, your interruption is for a worthwhile reason.

Don't get too cute with your subject line.

You're not spamming. You're not sending a pointless e-mail. There's no need, then, to trick a customer into reading what you're sending. That's not to say that you don't need to use a subject line that is attention-grabbing. Of course you do. Your subject line functions, more or less, as the headline for your e-mail. Still, it should reflect the content of your message fairly accurately and not be misleading. When in doubt, you should probably come down on the conservative side of the fence. After all, your e-mail marketing campaign, by definition, is part of an ongoing relationship with your customer. And the cost of each piece of e-mail is virtually nothing. If this particular e-mail gets trashed, that's fine. The important thing is to not get your recipient so ticked off at you that he or she opts out of your mailing list.

Be succinct.

Many of your customers get 30 or 40 e-mail messages a day. Some of them get many more. Once your message gets opened, the next trick is to get it read. Your chances increase dramatically if you're to-the-point. Remember, you just need to get their attention and interest in what you're offering. For those customers who are interested, you'll have links to a page on your Web site where they can find out everything they want to know. For those recipients who aren't interested, don't make them wade through several paragraphs to find out what you're talking about.

Make opt-out straightforward and easy.

Opt-out refers to the ability of someone who is on your list to indicate that they want to be removed. Making it easy to do so is simply a matter of courtesy and good business. After all, if someone doesn't want to be on your e-mail list, then whatever you send is immediately transformed into spam. Paradoxically, making it simple to get off will likely bolster the rate at which you retain people on your list rather than depress it. It's kind of like the Berlin Wall. Everyone anticipated that there'd be a mass exodus from East Berlin to West Berlin when the wall came down. Once the wall was down, though, there was no particular need for the people in East Berlin to leave. That may be a crude analogy, but the point is that your customers' comfort level in staying on your list will be much greater if they know that it's easy to get off the list if and when they want to.

Make it easy to reply to you.

The ideal situation is for your customer to be able to simply hit the "Reply" button in his or her e-mail program in order to get a message to you. If your Web people can't make that happen for some reason, then at least include a link in your e-mail messages that makes it easy to "talk" back to you. Your e-mail marketing becomes much more effective if you can turn it into an apparent or actual dialog. Don't let some obscure technical consideration stand between your company and your customers. If you are willing to intrude on someone's Inbox, then at least offer them the courtesy of making it easy to reply.

One last point about electronic communication. As I mentioned in Chapter 4, your Web site ought to prominently display a means for customers and prospects to contact you. This point may seem basic, but it is a point that somehow escapes many businesses. On those occasions when a customer contacts you, provide that customer with some kind of acknowledgment even if, for some reason, you cannot provide a personal reply.

It is surprising how many businesses fail to provide this simple courtesy (but it is not surprising how prominently that failure figures in customer dissatisfaction). Your Web team can implement an e-mail tool called an auto responder. As the name implies, it automatically responds to an e-mail message. It is obvious to your customer that it is the e-mail equivalent of the form letter, but automated responsiveness is better than personalized neglect.

Your auto responder message should clearly indicate to your customer what can be expected in the way of a personalized response. For example, you might say, "This is an automated response to your e-mail communication. We wanted to let you know that we received your message and will get back to you as quickly as possible. Currently, our response time is averaging approximately 48 hours. We appreciate your patience."

This is also a good practice to follow when someone orders something from your Web site. For example, *Photoaccess.com,* a Web site that offers photographic prints and novelty items from pictures taken with your digital camera, sends this e-mail message to a customer who places an order:

> *Your order has been received and is being processed. If you have any questions about your order please send us an e-mail message at orders@photoaccess.com (or just reply to this message) or call our toll-free number 1-888-871-7143 Monday through Friday 9 a.m. to 5 p.m. PST.*

That's pretty clear, and it covers all the bases mentioned in this chapter.

It should now be clear why e-mail marketing is such a powerful tool for communicating with your customers. But what if you could take it to the next level and send a personalized message to each and every one of your customers, even if there are millions of them? You can. You will in Chapter 8.

Chris Pirillo

Chris Pirillo is the author of Poor Richard's E-Mail Publishing, *as well as the publisher of* Lockergnome, *one of the most popular electronic newsletters on the Web.*

Colombo: Why does e-mail publishing in general, and electronic newsletters in particular, make sense as a marketing vehicle for small business?

Pirillo: Think about your own Internet habits. What is the first thing you do when you get online?

Colombo: I check my e-mail.

Pirillo: Thank you! In fact, that's probably what you do every five minutes, isn't it? There are a billion and one Web sites. Why on earth would you just sit there and wait for someone to come across your site? And why would you depend on them remembering to come back to your site? E-mail publishing is a much stronger vehicle for communication and that's what the Internet is all about: instant, digital, worldwide communication.

Colombo: It's about connecting with customers.

Pirillo: If you're trying to reach customers, e-mail is the best way—building a brand through e-mail. This is what a lot of people don't seem to understand. When you have a product or service and you're trying to get it out there, the big objective that you're going for is "branding." And that concept hasn't changed, even on the Internet. In fact, it's more important to brand on the Internet than it is offline. So, what people have forgotten in this search for the almighty click-through is that branding is critically important. As important as it is to get your ad on television and radio and billboards and in newspapers and magazines, it's just as important to find specific targeted advertising campaigns online. But instead of tracking cost per thousand (CPM), as in the traditional advertising world, companies are pursuing cost per action (CPA) and cost per click (CPC) models. That's a problem, because they forget about branding. It's not just about putting an ad there. It's about getting a well-wrapped sponsor message to a targeted audience, and there's no easier way of generating and continuing to generate a targeted audience than through e-mail.

Colombo: How do we define the distinction between e-mail and spam? And how do you make sure that you're on the right side of that?

Pirillo: It's about getting the users' permission. Not only getting their permission, but fully disclosing your privacy policy *before* they even sign up. By providing a double opt-in procedure—meaning that if you sign up online for an e-mail newsletter, you'd go to the Web site and sign up, but you would not actually be added to the distribution list until you replied to a message sent to that e-mail address basically saying, "You wanted to sign up for this, right?" Only *after* you say yes will you be added to the database. Most important, however, it's providing something that you said that you would provide. Making sure that you meet the users' expectations. They sign up for a list with the intent that you're going to send them X, Y, or Z, and as long as you deliver X, Y, or Z on a regular basis, you're good. They have to know what to expect even before they even open that message.

Now, to take that a step further: When you sit down and watch television, do you turn on the TV because you want to watch a program or commercial?

Colombo: Obviously you want to watch a program.

Pirillo: Let's take that into the e-mail world. When you sit down to read your e-mail, are you looking to be pitched or are you looking to be communicated to? You go to surf the Web; it requires your interaction. E-mail newsletters come to you. Once you sign up for my newsletter, I don't have to ask your permission every time I'm going to send out a new issue. I just send it to you. You've already given me your permission. I have to meet or exceed your expectations with quality content. Companies have to come across genuinely, they have to come across *regularly,* and they have to be personal. It's taking that extra step, because you are entering the most sacred place in the entire galaxy: someone's inbox.

Colombo: So there are other marketing efforts that precede and are wrapped around the e-mail marketing piece?

Pirillo: Oh, yeah. But make the clear distinction between e-mail marketing and e-mail publishing. Would you pick up a magazine over and over and over again if it had nothing but ads?

Colombo: No, you wouldn't.

Pirillo: *That* is e-mail marketing. E-mail publishing is *content.* Wrapped with a sponsor's message or a branding message. So let's say Joe's Garage has a Web site and wants to attract people to its place of business. Instead of sending out an e-mail every month saying, "Hey, we have a special going on, blah, blah, blah," wouldn't it be nice to have an auto care tips or a reminder about the next time your oil is due for a change?

Colombo: Right, and then you stay top-of-mind in that category. So how do you build the list?

Pirillo: First of all, *don't* rent a list. Don't purchase a list. Build it genuinely. How? Easy. You put it up on your Web site.

Colombo: And you make sure that there's a mechanism on your Web site to capture e-mail addresses.

Pirillo: My Web site has *three* subscription forms on the front page alone. I put a subscription form at the bottom of every page, because people scroll through a page and go to the very bottom to see what's down there. They see it and say, "Oh yeah, I guess I could subscribe" and they do. I put it in the sidebar in case they're looking there. So, it's not just a question of putting it on your site, but really wrapping your whole enterprise around it, because here's the question you've got to ask yourself: Are you willing to spend millions of dollars on your Web site and have nothing to keep people coming back?

This springboards to how you generate the list. You don't generate your list by asking a billion questions. If you ask too many questions, people won't sign up. In fact, you've lost 10 percent more of your customers.

Colombo: So the first piece of the answer to that question about capturing e-mail addresses is on your Web site. Any others?

Pirillo: The second way to build your list is to become an active member in the community.

Colombo: Whichever community you're doing business in, whether you define it geographically or vertically or however?

Pirillo: Even online. Go into a newsgroup or a bulletin board and if someone has a question about a product or a service, answer the question. Don't push your Web site, just answer the question. Let people warm up to who you are. You're not there to hawk a product. And then, after you become a regular, maybe you could put your company's URL on your signature. It's a targeted way of doing things. You get your name in front of people so that you establish trust. You have to become an active member and provide a benefit above and beyond what everyone else is providing.

Colombo: You have to *earn* your way in.

Pirillo: This ties back in to the *best* form of marketing: word of mouth, because you will generate so much response.

Colombo: Word of mouth is totally credible.

Pirillo: It adds 1,000-percent credibility to whatever you're doing. I get a lot of new subscribers to my e-mail *Lockergnome* on a daily basis, and I prefer people to come in through friends because they know what to expect. They say, "Well, Bill likes it. I'm going to like, too." They're automatically set up in that mindset, and that's what you want. You want to be approachable and build on that. It's not just adding subscribers to your list. It's adding *value* for your subscribers because then they will double, triple, quadruple your value over time. Make an investment in the subscribers that you currently have. You have to cultivate a true personal relationship with them. Their recommendation goes a long way.

Colombo: And do you need to subtly plant the idea that recommending you to somebody else is a good thing to do?

Pirillo: Yes! Just come out and ask them, "Hey, can you recommend me to a friend?" I'll just say, "We're having a contest and giving away licenses of some product. Recommend us to a friend." I'll get 5,000 recommendations in a week. This is phenomenal.

Colombo: Absolutely. Would it be accurate to say that the nature of this medium is narrowcasting rather than broadcasting?

Pirillo: I'd say it's a combination of both. E-mail is widely used. It is a broadcast medium. However, when you're talking about e-mail publishing, you're talking about targeting a certain demographic. Think of it as an e-mail newsletter. Those are targeted. That's narrowcasting.

Colombo: So you need to know exactly who your target is and, just as important, who it isn't?

Pirillo: You have to know your audience.

Colombo: The point I'm trying to make is that it's hard to be meaningful in a general way. You can only be meaningful in a specific way in this type of medium.

Pirillo: Think about your audience. You've got to pander to that group.

Colombo: In describing the content, you said that it needs to be genuine and personal. Is it important to not sound corporate in your communications?

Pirillo: It is *so* important, because e-mail is a *personal* medium. When you sit down to write e-mail, you're expecting personal correspondence; you want to interact with somebody. You do not want to hear corporate blah, blah, blah.

Colombo: I think there is an almost irresistible tendency to use bland, corporate communication. Marketers are so used to doing that in terms of business communication. How do you get out of that mode?

Pirillo: Use your own voice. Don't send me a marketing pitch. You have a great product or service. If it's great, it will speak for itself. Don't tell me what it will do for my life. Just show it to me and ask me what I think. You'll get a lot further that way, because you're requiring mental interaction that develops a personal relationship. I hate marketers, because they don't get it. I'll ask them a question and they'll give me a positioning statement. I'm not going to listen to it! They've lost me, and they've lost 90 percent of the people out there.

Colombo: It's interesting that in a high-tech environment, the element of personalization is maybe even more important than it is elsewhere. This goes back to a point that you made earlier about how there is almost an irrational reaction that people have when they feel like their e-mail is being violated.

Pirillo: It's the holiest of all holy places. You can come up to somebody, you can hand them a flyer and it doesn't affect them. You do the same thing in the Inbox and you're *dead*. You probably heard another term being tossed around called viral marketing? [Viral marketing is a systemized, specialized method of creating what used to be known as word-of-mouth. A positive marketing message is passed from one person to another the way a virus can be.] It's a sham because it's always going to be up to the people. You can prepare for it, but I guarantee it, there is nothing that you could do to make something like that happen. It either happens or it doesn't. If your product or service is valid, there's a *possibility* of that happening.

That can come around and bite you. Have you ever heard of this company called All Advantage? What they had was a get-paid-to-surf program. Well, that was viral. It was all over the place overnight. Everybody was signing up. The problem was that the advertising market changed from a CPM to a more CPA or CPC approach. They had to cut back their prices and their hours and they couldn't pay their users enough.

Colombo: And there was a huge backlash.

Pirillo: Major. It's an example of reverse viral marketing. There's probably no way they're going to survive. They lost about half of their customer base. People were so frustrated with the way they handled the situation.

Colombo: Negative viral is probably faster than positive viral and more powerful.

Pirillo: It is, because people accentuate the negative. The last thing you want to do is offend users. If they can't get help from you, if they're looking for something that you're not giving them that you'd said you'd give them, that's a problem. As long as you meet their expectations, it's fine.

Chapter 8

Mass Personalizing Your Communications

Comedian Steve Martin used to end his stand-up routine by saying, "I'd like to thank each and every one of you for being here this evening." Then, he'd start pointing to one member of the audience at a time and, with a lightening fast delivery, do exactly what he said he was going to do: thank each member of the audience, one at a time. "Thank you, thank you, thank you, thank you, thank you, thank you, thank you, thank you, thank you, thank you, thank you, thank you, thank you...."

Funny stuff. But the truth is that technology now gives you the power to basically do precisely what Martin joked about. You can individually communicate with each and every one of your customers. Even if you have thousands of them, or even millions. Actually, you can do even more than that. You can "talk" to each customer with a message that you've carefully designed specifically for him or her.

In fact, if you're interested in raising your company's marketing effectiveness to the next level, you cannot afford to stay stuck at the level of mass communication. You've got to move your communications down to an entirely different level of granularity. And technology provides you with the tools to do precisely that. The object of your efforts is to be able to make your customers think, "Wow! They're talking to me!" Once you can do that, you've got their undivided attention and you've established a significant amount of credibility.

Attention and Credibility

You've got their attention because you've targeted your message in a way that almost makes it impossible to ignore. Customers and prospects have, over the years, become amazingly adept at tuning out what they perceive to be "noise" in the marketplace. It would be almost impossible to function otherwise. Most people are, during the course of a typical day, bombarded with hundreds of sales and marketing messages. There simply isn't time to pay attention to each one.

Personalization is an extremely effective strategy for differentiating your message in a "noisy" environment. Customers are likely to pay attention to something that seems to be theirs and theirs alone. Use of your customer's name in your message is a starting point, of course, but don't kid yourself. It is no more than a starting point. Customers have seen enough "personalized" direct mail pieces to understand how that deal works. If you're going to really get someone's attention, your personalization is going to have to go beyond the superficial. (In just a moment, you'll see what I mean.)

In addition to getting your customer's attention, though, personalizing your message will help you to achieve a high degree of credibility. If you think about your own experience as a customer or client, it's not hard to see how this works. Let's say that you're the owner of a small business. Consider what it would be like to be on the receiving end of two sales calls, both from insurance agents who want to sell you group health insurance. The first agent talks to you about "our three plans that are most popular among small businesses in this area." The second agent, in contrast, says, "I've taken the liberty of doing a little research on your business. I know that you've got 15 employees, and that five of them work part-time. I also know that you're organized as a Sub-Chapter 'S' corporation. Based on that information, I put together a spreadsheet showing...." Which of these two is more credible? No question about it. The second agent has so much more credibility that it's not even close.

In addition to the obvious, there's something else worth noting about the difference between these two presentations. It's that the first agent didn't go in completely oblivious to your situation. In fact, he went so far as to narrow your choices down to ones that were popular with other small businesses and with other businesses in your area. Compared to starting from scratch, that would seem to be fairly specific proposal. Yet, ultimately it looks pretty weak when compared to an offer that's truly personalized.

Laying the Groundwork

What's the key to personalizing communications? It's information. Look at it this way. If you had no information about a particular prospect, there'd be no chance at all of personalizing a marketing message. You'd be reduced to either talking about your product or service in and of itself (yawn!) or you'd have to make a few educated guesses about what might be interesting or beneficial to the person you were talking to. If you knew a little bit about that person, you'd be able to focus your message a little more. But if you knew a great deal about your prospect, then you could get extremely specific and craft a presentation that was extremely personalized.

So, where can you get the information you need? Turn back to Chapter 5 and you'll see that you ought to be building information gathering processes into *all* of your customer interactions, online and off. What you need to do is make sure that all of the information you've gathered gets entered into a database. That database will become, over time, the most valuable asset your company owns.

You can use a general purpose database, such as Microsoft Access, if you'd like, but most businesses are better off with a database program that is specifically designed to handle customer information and manage customer interactions. They generally fall into the category of customer relationship management (CRM) software. Some of the more popular packages for small and medium-sized businesses include:

@   Goldmine (*Goldmine.com*).

@   SalesLogix (*Saleslogix.com*).

@   Pivotal (*Pivotal.com*).

These programs, and others like them, come ready to use and include a variety of sales and marketing functions already built in. They can be used by salespeople in a store or sales office who are connected to a network, but they can also be used by your salespeople in the field. And they can integrate with whatever you're doing on the Web. For the purposes of our discussion in this chapter, though, the important thing to know is that they can be used to generate and manage a variety of personalized customer communications.

The basic model is to gather information from your customers as you interact with them over time, and then to make sure that information is recorded in a database program. In Chapter 5, we discussed the fact that customer contact information needs to be the starting point of your information gathering efforts, but our discussion so far in this chapter ought to be making it clear that you want much more information than just the customer's name, address, phone number, and e-mail address. As we've seen, your communication can only be personalized to the degree that you have access to all kinds of customer information. The specific information you'll want to keep track of depends on the nature of your business, but the general idea is to track information that you can use to usefully segment your customer list. Here are a just few ideas that you might want to consider:

For Business Clients:

@ Industry (SIC code).

@ Number of employees.

@ Approximate gross sales volume.

@ Ownership (public or private).

@ Business type (retail, manufacturer, etc.).

@ Referral source.

@ Purchasing history.

For Individual Consumers:

@ Gender.

@ Marital status.

@ Parenthood status.

@ Home ownership.

@ Hobbies.

@ Referral source.

@ Pet ownership.

These lists are certainly not comprehensive. They're meant to get you thinking of ways in which a customer list might be sorted. If you think about it, I'm sure you'll have no trouble at all coming up with categories that are relevant to your particular business and customer lists. Once you have your own categories, then you'll find yourself looking at all sorts of intriguing opportunities for personalized communications.

Let's use the categories that I've just listed to give you a better idea of what I'm talking about. As an example, let's say you're in the real estate business. If you were tracking these categories for your customers and prospects, think how your marketing communications might differ for customers who are married men with children and are homeowners versus unmarried women with no children who rent.

It should be obvious that almost everything about your message to prospects in the first category would differ from a message you might send to prospects in the second category. For the first group, your message might include things such as:

@ What a great time it is to sell an existing home and trade up.

@ The terrific schools that are found in the neighborhoods you specialize in.

@ Moving companies you work with that can move an entire household easily and inexpensively.

@ The attractive arrangements you're able to offer for someone who both lists with you and buys from you.

Those are all great selling points, but they are likely to be less than meaningful to prospects in the second category. For those prospects, you might want to talk about:

@ The economic advantages of home ownership versus renting.

@ Favorable financing that you can offer to first time buyers.

@ The safety and security of the neighborhoods you specialize in.

@ The fact that you have a large number of newer homes listed at the moment that are in great condition and won't need any work when the new owner moves in.

In each of these examples, once you have segmented your customer list, you are able to create a marketing communication that focuses in on the needs and wants of each sub-group with a high degree of precision.

Your Message

A term that's often used to describe this close alignment of your marketing message with its intended recipient is message-to-market match. In the past, it was possible to do this in only the broadest terms. Technology today makes it possible for you to execute this highly effective technique with a much finer degree of granularity than was ever possible before—and at a lower cost than ever before.

The payoff for you as a marketer is tremendous. You will increase the response rate for your offers because you're focusing your message on benefits that are specifically matched to its recipient. In other words, you're using the right bait for the specific fish you're after. A well-maintained customer database will allow you to strengthen the bond between you and your customers significantly. You'll find that the sharpness of the focus that you bring to your customer base will translate into a stronger sense of connection between you and your customers and prospects. Targeted, personalized communication will give each customer a reason to think, "They're speaking my language. They really understand what's important to me."

Although a special sales offer is the most obvious reason to communicate, there are others. For example, there might be service information on a particular product that you can communicate to your customers who bought it. Or there might be a complimentary product that is new to the market. Or you might communicate with customers about the status of their warranty or service agreements. All of these are great reasons to stay in touch with your customers. And all of them represent an opportunity for you to add value to the relationship. All of them are important steps in the ongoing process of capturing customers.

Pick Your Medium

Once you've created the foundation for this kind of customer communication, you'll find yourself with a tremendous amount of flexibility. Your customer database will be versatile and powerful enough to take you anywhere you want to go.

In the previous chapter, I discussed electronic mail at length and explained its advantages as a customer communications medium. It's important to note that although all of that is true, it's also true that there are other ways to communicate with your customers and prospects. You should be using them all. The good news, though, is that your customer information system, and the strategy of personalizing your communications, will be just as effective no matter which medium you choose.

All of the principles of personalization that I've discussed here will obviously work when communication takes place by e-mail, but they are just as effective when they're implemented in conjunction with other media.

Your CRM software, along with a fax modem, can handle a broadcast fax just as easily as it can handle electronic mail. Although fax does not seem to have the same cache that e-mail has, it can be just as inexpensive and just as effective—maybe even more so, depending on your market. In some markets, where e-mail is becoming pervasive, a fax will stand out if for no other reason then because it is unusual. In other markets, e-mail might not yet be as widely adopted as fax.

You will also occasionally want to make use of traditional mail pieces as part of your customer communications mix. Sure, it's slow and expensive, but it will sometimes be able to deliver your message with an impact that is not available any other way. And don't overlook the possibility of mixing media with an integrated message. You might use e-mail to "tease" a snail mail package that you're going to send, for example.

A Personalized Electronic Environment

Up until now, we've discussed the personalization of outgoing communications. Another personalization opportunity exists on your Web site. It is possible to customize the page that a client sees when he or she logs on to your Web site. One possibility is to tie your Web site to your customer database and automatically deliver information that's tailored to meet your client's interests or to reflect his or her purchasing history. Again, we can turn to *Amazon.com* for an instructive example. When I log on to Amazon, the start page I see is different from the one you see when you log on. It features books that are likely to be of interest to me based on my purchasing history. Such personalization can reflect anything you want, though, depending on what content is available on your site and what information you track for each customer.

Going back to the real estate example that I used earlier, if you're in that business and maintain a Web site, you might offer current homeowners a start screen that will link them to a "trade-up" calculator. Prospects who are currently renters, on the other hand, might get a start screen with a series of frequently asked questions for first-time buyers. Members of each group, then, would wind up perceiving you as a specialist in the particular area that interests them.

Another approach would be to allow your client to pick and choose from among various informational elements that she wants to see when she logs on. Financial Web sites do this when they allow a client to populate her start page with stock prices from the particular stocks that are in her portfolio. This approach actively involves your client in the customization process.

In fact, the principle of putting control of various aspects of the selling and marketing process in the hands of your customers is an important one. It's so important, in fact, that Chapter 9 is devoted to it.

Don Peppers

Don is a partner at Peppers and Rogers Group, a management consulting firm with offices throughout the United States as well as in Europe, Latin America, and South Africa. He is the co-author of several highly acclaimed business books on the subject of customer relationship management, including The One to One Future, *which introduced the phrase "one-to-one marketing."*

Colombo: Let's start with the basics. Can you give an overview of one-to-one marketing?

Peppers: Sure. One-to-one marketing is based on creating individual relationships with individual customers, treating different customers differently. What's necessary to create that kind of relationship is a database of customer information. You have to know who your customers are—their identities and how to get in touch with them and so forth. You have to be able to interact with the customers. That is, the relationship is interactive and so on your Web site, in your call center, in your sales force automation tool, on your point of purchase—wherever—that information has to captured by you. And you have to be not only able, but also willing to actually tailor your behavior in some way to the individual needs of an individual customer. That's what allows you to set up that interactive, long-term relationship, which we call a *learning relationship*. A relationship with the customer that gets smarter and smarter with every interaction. So, if I can interact and I'm tracking you and I can customize, then you tell me what you want and then I make it for you. And then we interact again. "Did you like it that way? Do you want it more this way next time? How about that?" I get a little higher up your learning curve and my product has more value to you and I'm making it more convenient for you to remain loyal to me rather than go to my competitor and re-teach him what you've already taught me. And *that's* the real power of one-to-one marketing.

Colombo: It really captures the customer. It makes the barriers to entry for your competitors prohibitive because, if you have that kind of information, how does the competitor ever get there?

Peppers: Exactly. As long as you maintain product and service quality that is at least on par with your competitors, then having this personalized relationship with the individual customer means that the customer's interest is best served by remaining loyal. The flip side of that is that your unit margins are going to improve, because the reason margins are under pressure in most businesses is competitive pricing. Your competitor comes in a market, undercuts your price, and you have to match to keep your customers. So he cuts again, and pretty soon your margins are falling. But, if you could make it more convenient for your customer to remain loyal than to go someplace else, then you don't necessarily have to meet 100 percent of your competitor's discounts.

Colombo: What companies are doing this particularly well?

Peppers: Let me give a few quick examples. The first is Peapod (*www.peapod.com*), the online grocery delivery service. There are 30,000 products you could choose from to order groceries online and then they bring them to your house. But the second week, when you sign on, you don't stroll down their aisles and click on their groceries again. You start by calling up your last week's shopping list. And you make changes. And then the week after that, the list is better. And every week it's easier. In just a few weeks on the program, most Peapod customers do their week's worth of shopping in just a few minutes. And that's a classic *learning relationship* dynamic. Another example is *Amazon.com*'s book matching, the ability to plot the books that you've bought in the past with the books you've expressed an interest in, and then make recommendations to you. So that the more you've interacted with Amazon, the easier it is for you to find the books that you want. And of course, the next step for them is going to be you scheduling the book deliveries: Next time their sponsor comes out with a book, I want you to send it to me—on an automated basis.

British Airways (*www.britishairways.com*) has installed software that allows it to track on-board amenities down to the level of the individual customer on its trans-Atlantic flights. So when I get on a British Airways flight to London in a few months, they might say to me, "Welcome back, Mr. Peppers, we have your caffeine-free Diet Coke on board."

What's necessary to do that, of course, is they have to have information from me, they have to have interacted with me to get that information. Probably they did that during my last flight. And, in fact, they've installed PCs in the galleys of the first- and business-class sections of their trans-Atlantic flights, so that when a flight attendant in his or her judgement thinks that the customer has given some important information about their personal preferences, they input that into the database under that passenger's name. And they already know your name because you're on the frequent flyer program, you're on the [flight] manifest, and so forth. So they've identified their customers. They've also figured out how to mass-customize their on-board provisioning.

Mass-customization is a key issue here, because you're going to go out of business if you pay to customize everything. Right now, it only really pays to customize products for very valuable customers or to customize complex, expensive products. But, in a mass-marketing world, and in a world of thousands or millions of customers, you have to come up with streamlined ways to tailor products. And mass-customization is really the computerized standardization of products. Everybody has read about Levi's personal pair of jeans program, in which it produces ten thousand different sizes of women's jeans on one assembly line. Well, the way they do that is they pre-manufacture 400 hip sizes and 30 legs sizes then match your hips to your legs. So, the mass-customizer reduces his behavior, his production process, or his service delivery process to modules and then digitally configures the modules. And the more modules you have, the more granularity there is, the more possible number of fits you offer.

Colombo: It would seem to me that companies that do this right, create for themselves an overwhelming competitive advantage in the marketplace. So why isn't everybody doing this?

Peppers: Well, there are lots of obstacles. This is a different dimension of competition. The traditional marketer tries to find more customers for the product he's trying to sell. But the one-to-one marketer is trying to find more products and services for the customers whose needs he's serving. The one-to-one marketer focuses on share of customer, not just market share, which is a product-based metric. Unfortunately, almost all companies today are organized on the product dimension, not the customer dimension. We have a division that produces

Product A and a division that produces Product B. We don't have divisions that handle each type of customer across all products. In fact, when you think about your business in the customer dimension, you have to cross divisional and functional lines.

Colombo: How can you achieve this customer dimension?

Peppers: There are a few types of integration involved in this. One is functional integration. If you tell me what you want, and I make it for you, that implies that the back end of my company has to be willing and able to conform to what the front end learns that an individual customer wants. Production and marketing have to be highly coordinated. To you, we're the same company; to us, you ought to be the same customer. There are a lot of cross-divisional boundaries involved there. Another kind of integration is a trans-enterprise integration. I'll give you an example. If you're a home builder and I come to you to have my home built, you know that I need a realtor, an insurance agent, a mortgage broker, a surveyor, an architect, and an insurance company. All these are part of an integrated solution to my problem, which is getting a house built. But the only part of that solution that you actually sell yourself is the home building. However, even though you don't want to become a realtor or a mortgage broker, it would pay you to have a strategic alliance with firms that can solve these needs, because if you have confidence in a sister firm or an alliance firm that can solve your customer's problems, then you are able to retain a larger share of that customer's business. You can broker the customer's needs.

Colombo: So, the primary impediments for companies that want to get to this one-to-one future, to coin a phrase, are really social and political rather than technological.

Peppers: Yes. They're organizational and they're cultural and a lot of times they involve metrics. For example, the marketing budget is a function of how many new customers we acquire.

But to acquire customers who stay longer, we should acquire fewer customers but better customers. When MCI tried to implement a customer loyalty program, the effort failed because it hadn't reset the metrics in the marketing department. Marketing says, "Wait a minute! We're acquiring fewer customers. That means my budget goes down, and I don't like that."

Colombo: Would it be fair to say, then, that for this kind of effort to be successful, it really has to be driven by the top of the organization?

Peppers: *Exactly*. These issues of enterprise integration are not things that can be resolved without the active endorsement and maybe participation of the CEO.

One of the interesting things that's going on today on Web sites is that when a traditionally organized company begins thinking of putting up a Web site to interact with customers, right away a different kind of marketing is required. Suddenly you are able to create interactive one-to-one relationships with individual customers and that immediately raises all those organizational conflicts. That's why putting together a really first class Web site for a large enterprise can often serve as a kind of a crucible to hammer out all the conflicts that exist at the divisional level. And if an organization is able to put together a customer-specific, one-to-one, customized Web site across different divisions, then it has been able to resolve those conflicts. You can literally take the policies that you're applying on your Web site and apply them across divisions.

Colombo: That's great. Let's talk about the components that you mentioned at the outset of one-to-one marketing. What should companies be thinking about to do a database correctly?

Peppers: A lot of firms say they know their customers. Well, what they really mean is they know the profile of their average customers and they may have sophisticated models of different types of customers. The database means that you need to capture the addressable identity of an individual customer. And you need to use the information in the database to begin to differentiate your customers, one from another, in terms of what's important to you.

Colombo: But the average doesn't say anything about the individual.

Peppers: No. If you want to create a relationship with somebody, it has to be a specific relationship with a particular person. And if you don't know who that person is, then you can't create the relationship.

Colombo: What do you need to know?

Peppers: There are two aspects of customer differences that are important to the enterprising. The first is what the customer is worth to the enterprise, because some customers are worth a lot and some aren't worth so much. So the value of the customer, which would be the sum total of his future profit stream with you discounted to the present, is an important differentiator.

The second way customers are different is they need different things from you. So what a customer wants and what he's worth to you, that's both sides of the value proposition.

Colombo: How does the database fit in?

Peppers: You use your database to track transactions, to analyze the data, and basically to try to understand the nature of your customers. And in fact, the customer base itself can be characterized by the degree of differences within the customer base. So, for instance, if I want to set a learning relationship with my customers, the real power of that relationship is that the customer is going to find it more convenient to keep dealing with me rather than teach somebody else what I've already learned. That leverage increases the more what the customer needs is different from what every other customer needs. Take a bookstore. There are tens of thousands of books in the bookstore. Everybody needs a different book. Everybody has different tastes. Everybody needs something different. So, if you went into the bookstore and they said, "Welcome back, Mr. Peppers. I know you like Elmore Leonard. Since you were last in, Elmore Leonard came out with a new novel, so I put it aside." I'd be very loyal to that bookstore. Contrast the bookstore however with, say, a gas station. There are three or four types of gasoline. Say I went into the gas station, and they said, "Welcome back, Mr. Peppers. We've got a new shipment of 93 octane, just the way you like it!" That's not exactly a compelling benefit.

The more different your customers are in terms of what they need, the more powerful the idea of creating a learning relationship can be.

Colombo: Are there other ways you can differentiate?

Peppers: Yes. If your customers aren't different in terms of what they need, then you need to expand the definition of your product or your service. Expand the definition of your customers' needs: Differentiate the invoicing, the cost-control reports, and the instruction manuals; differentiate the way you package or palatize the product, the shipping and logistics behind it; add products; create alliances with other firms and differentiate that.

Colombo: So those become the ways that we take the database and move to step two, which is to interact individually.

Peppers: Right. Interaction is an important driver of this, because the customer may not be explicitly aware of the data that you have about him, but he's definitely aware once you interact with him.

The two key principles to remember are cost efficiency and effectiveness. Cost efficiency means you want to drive as many interactions as you can into more and more cost-efficient media. Automate the sales force so that the manual sales call can more efficiently capture the customer's interaction. Drive sales calls into the call center to the extent you can. Drive call interactions to your Web site. Create self-help mechanisms for customers to find it in their interest to interact in an automated fashion. Not so you can reduce the human element, but so that you can afford to do more interaction with more customers and capture this information in a cost-efficient manner.

Effectiveness means the interaction you want is one that allows you to gather information from a customer that will be useful to you in strengthening and deepening your relationship with him. You want to be gathering information you may not be able to get from some other source or information that the customer has an investment in giving you. You want the customer to be involved in a relationship. It's his involvement, his investment in the relationship that leads to his wanting to remain loyal.

Colombo: And as you get more of that information, your database becomes better, you can differentiate among customers better. It's cyclical.

Peppers: Exactly. And there's an interesting parallel between your interactive capacity and customer differentiation. The more different customers are in their needs, the better the learning relationship works. The more different customers are in terms of their value, the more cost efficient it is to practice one-to-one marketing. If I have a steep value skew, if the top 2 percent of my customers do 50 percent of my profit, then I can protect 50 percent of my profit by finding that top 2 percent of customers and making them loyal. But if my skew is more shallow, if it's the top 20 percent of my customers that do 50 percent of my profit, it's 10 times as costly for me to have the same effect on my bottom line.

Colombo: Right.

Peppers: Let me go back to the bookstore example. The reason the bookstore proprietor does not say to me, "Welcome back.

Elmore Leonard has a new novel out," is that it's not cost efficient for him to do so. Even if he were to memorize his top 100 customers, the proportion of business that he would affect by doing that is minuscule. But *Amazon.com,* by creating an interactive mechanism to cost efficiently track customers, can do exactly that. And they really do say, "Welcome back, Mr. Peppers. Elmore Leonard has a new novel out." And they say it not just for their top hundred customers, but for thousands of customers. And they're able to create that one-to-one relationship.

Colombo: How does mass-customization fit in?

Peppers: Go back to the Levi's example, which shows how mass-customization is different from customization. They could have posted a tailor at every one of their stores and the tailor would take individual customer measurements and make the jeans to their size right there. Of course, that would have been expensive and made it difficult for Levi Strauss to control the quality of those products. Customers would have ended up less satisfied had that been the solution. It's a lot easier for Levi Strauss to precisely control the digitized manufacturing of a product than to control the customization of a product. So mass-customization technologies are important to understand in order to practice one-to-one marketing. Levi's unit costs for producing customized blue jeans are actually lower—that is, its cost per pair of customized jeans is lower than the cost of non-custom jeans. Primarily because they have no inventory risk. You only make a pair of jeans when you already have a customer.

Colombo: So there's higher quality and higher perceived value to the customer and at the same time, the overall costs are lower?

Peppers: In many applications, lowered real costs and operating costs. And this combination of more efficient production process with a better fitting product for your customer and a more satisfied customer permeates the world of one-to-one marketing.

Chapter 9

The Self-Service Imperative

●

ATM terminals have become so much a part of our day-to-day lives that it's difficult to imagine not having one nearby. But, of course, they weren't always around. In fact, the first ATMs did not appear in the United States until 1969, a couple of years after their debut in the U.K. And although they certainly seem indispensable today, it's amazing to note that it was not entirely clear at the time that the banking public was going to embrace these new contraptions.

For one thing, lots of people didn't trust them or the computerized accounting behind them. Everyone had heard stories of an outlandish mistake on a friend's or neighbor's bank statement that was a nightmare to straighten out. Besides, why in the world would anyone use a machine when they could step into the bank (almost all ATMs were located at banks at that time) and get personalized service from a teller? It just didn't seem to make sense.

What happened? As ATMs began to appear in places besides banks, convenience certainly became a factor. In addition to the convenience of non-bank locations, however, one other factor about using ATMs turned out to be significant: the ability of customers to conduct their own transactions. As it turns out, the proliferation of ATMs was a harbinger of things to come. We know now that the self-service imperative has become one of the most important success factors of today's Internet-driven business environment. Simply put, customers want their finger—not yours or your employee's—on the "Enter" key for their transactions.

When you think about it, every Web site, by definition, is a self-service operation. The basic business proposition behind many Web sites is to attract users based on offering self-service in areas for which it has never before been available. But the Web is not the only place where self-service makes sense.

Success Factors for Self-Service

Before you rush off and try to implement some sort of self-service in all of your customer interactions, though, let's take a look at three critical success factors that you're going to want to keep in mind when it comes to delivering self-service: reliability, use interface, and feedback loop.

Reliability

Looking back on the example of ATMs, we know that skepticism about the reliability of the machines and the accuracy of the transactions was a factor that significantly impeded their adoption during the first few years of their existence. The rule here is pretty straightforward: Customers will avoid a self-service system that they don't trust. They don't want to spend time entering an order, for example, only to have it returned for some nit-picky reason. If they believe that might turn out to be the case, then they'd rather enlist the aid of one of your employees (on the phone or in person) to get it done.

This rule is certainly true as it relates to your customers' convenience. When we're talking about their money, though, the stakes are even higher. When anything having to do with their money is involved, your customers have to believe that your system is bullet-proof before they're going to be willing to embrace it. At my local supermarket, for example, there's a self-service checkout line that allows customers to scan their own orders. In my experience, something goes wrong once out of every four or five times I try to use it. So, I've given up. I regularly wait in line for a regular checkout counter rather than take a chance with this mess. (I'm not the only one, either. The self-service checkout line at this store is typically empty— which is a good indication, by the way, that this particular self-service system has failed!)

Privacy and security can be elements of reliability, and these subjects are so important that they merit their own discussion. I'll talk about them at length in Chapter 13.

User Interface

This is a term that refers to the ways in which your customers interact with your self-service systems. A user interface can be friendly and intuitive or it can be difficult and confusing. The ideal user interface needs little instruction or explanation and allows the user to accomplish something with a minimum amount of time and effort. Usually, there's an inverse relationship between a system's complexity and the elegance of its user interface.

It's often assumed that graphical elements make a user interface easier. That's not necessarily true. Many elevators, for example, use little pictures (icons) to indicate "open" and "closed." As many times as I've seen those same icons, the doors have usually decided what to do on their own before I can remember which one is which. This is a situation where, at least for me, words would be a lot more straightforward than icons.

Customers will be more likely to use any kind of self-service system if it has a friendly user interface. Back at my local supermarket for a moment, the user interface of the credit card machine is an example of a particularly bad design. Just figuring out how to swipe the credit card in order to get started is a challenge, and it gets worse from there. The poor design is betrayed by the fact that the cashiers immediately begin coaching you through the steps when you pull out a credit card. That indicates that they almost always wind up getting asked for help— another sign of a failed self-service system.

Feedback Loop

This is an element of the user interface, but it's so important— and so often overlooked—that I wanted to mention it separately.

A feedback loop tells the user whether something he or she was trying to accomplish worked or not. Let's go back to a typical elevator for a simple example. What would you think if you pressed the button to go to the seventh floor and there was no light on or near the button? You wouldn't know what to think. You'd have no idea whether or not the elevator got the message to take you to the seventh floor. You'd have no feedback.

When a customer is using a self-service system, he or she needs feedback that any choices that were made during the use of the system were made correctly and accepted by the system. That's what a feedback loop provides.

More About Usability

It was back in the early 1980s when one of the most dominant companies in the industry announced a breakthrough product designed to revolutionize the entire software environment for users of IBM-compatible personal computers. The radical concept behind the product was to give users a graphical user interface that would replace the text-based DOS interface that was then the industry standard. Applications programs would run inside of windows that appeared on the screen and users would navigate through their various tasks with a pointing device called a mouse.

Obviously, this is a synopsis of one of the most famous success stories in the history of the computer industry, right? Not exactly. It's actually the story of a company called VisiCorp, one of the most successful software companies of its day. It dominated the software industry with a product called VisiCalc. The revolutionary product that VisiCorp introduced (amidst enormous amounts of fanfare and hype) was called VisiOn—and it turned out to be anything but a "can't miss" idea. No more than a minor footnote in the history of the industry, VisiOn serves today as an illustration of a principle that is tremendously important but often overlooked: In the world of technology, the penalty for being too early is often greater than the penalty for being too late.

What does this mean to you? It's a principle that you ought to keep in mind the next time your Web consultant badgers you about adopting some gaudy bit of new technology for your company's Web site. If you get too far out in front of your customers with bleeding edge technology, your Web site and your business are going to suffer for it.

A recent survey by the Boston Consulting Group identified the reasons most often cited by online shoppers who had given up on one or more attempted purchases. Three of the top four responses are characteristic of Web sites that are too technologically sophisticated for their own good. More than one fourth of respondents left because a site crashed during an attempted purchase. Almost half gave up because a site was too confusing. And an even greater number bailed out when a site took too long to load.

In other words, the admonitions of your Web consultant notwithstanding, the behavior of actual consumers demonstrates that stability, simplicity, and responsiveness are the qualities that make for a successful Web site. These are all qualities that are compromised when you venture too far out in front of mainstream Web technology. All of the latest and greatest plug-ins might keep your Web consultant gainfully employed and might even win design awards, but there's no evidence that they do anything at all to increase your sales or enhance the quality of your customer's experience. This is especially true if your site is aimed at the consumer marketplace, where a sizeable segment of your visitors are surfing the Internet with training wheels (that is, they're using America Online).

Web design expert Jakob Nielsen has a great deal to say about usability and design issues on his Web site (*Useit.com*). Nielsen's approach might be a little *too* austere, but his underlying message is one you should consider: Don't let gaudy technology get in between you and your user.

When your customers are ready, you can implement whichever proven Web technologies you choose. In the meantime, though, if your competitors want to push the envelope, that's fine. They can pay the price of interrupted site visits and lost visitors.

Buying, Not Being Sold To

What does all of this mean in the world of selling and marketing? It means that your customers are more likely to buy, they're more likely to buy more, and they're more likely to buy more often if you can provide them with a buying experience in which they feel that they're in charge, that they're controlling the various elements of the selling situation. They want to feel as though you're not selling, but rather they're buying.

A classic example of this was recorded in a video based on Tom Peters' classic, *In Search of Excellence*. A scene in the video was shot at Stew Leonard's legendary grocery store in Norwalk. In this particular scene, Stew Leonard, Jr. was illustrating how the store tries to offer self-service in addition to prepackaged options. Leonard illustrated his line of reasoning by pointing out a shopper who was filling a container with strawberries. "She probably doesn't realize it, but she's got about 12 or 13 dollars worth of strawberries there!" he explained.

Examples of how customers have embraced the self-service concept when it's offered aren't hard to find:

@   In New York's La Guardia Airport, fliers on Delta's Shuttle to Boston or Washington, D.C. can buy their tickets from a vending machine right there at the terminal.

@   Discount brokers that allow customers to manage their own stock portfolios continue to flourish.

@   At Target stores, terminals are located throughout each store that allow a customer to scan bar codes on merchandise to get pricing information.

@   American Express allows its cardholders to manage many elements of their account themselves, utilizing the keypad of a touchtone phone.

@   At many photo-processing outlets, Kodak offers self-service kiosks that allow customers to enlarge, crop, and duplicate their own photos.

Of course, as I mentioned at the beginning of this chapter, the Web represents the biggest self-service explosion of all. Web technology allows elements of self-service to be incorporated into sales (buying) situations where it was never before possible.

An important ancillary benefit of self-service, by the way, is that it lowers your costs over time, because your customers are taking over functions that used to have to be handled by employees. You're enhancing your customer's experience, increasing customer satisfaction, and lowering costs all at the same time.

Elements of Self-Service

How can you take advantage of your customers' innate inclination toward self-service in your business? Start by looking for elements of your selling process where your salespeople or associates either don't add value or where they actually interfere with the task at hand but can't figure out how to get out of the way. Also, see if you can identify situations where your customers regularly become impatient with your employees or where they're forced to wait for some employee intervention to do something that could otherwise be accomplished themselves. Here are some ideas and principles that should get you started:

Let your customers "own" their customer profiles.

If you're keeping records of contact information and other useful customer information, why not get your customers involved in both the creation and maintenance of that information? On a Web site, implementing this principle is a no-brainer, but you can just as easily do it if you have a sales office or store. In Chapter 12, you'll see how you can create incentives that will make your customers actually clamor to do this. In a store or sales office, you can have terminals available that will let a customer create and/or edit his or her customer profile. Or, even if you're not doing e-commerce, you can still give customers the option of creating and managing their customer profiles over the Web.

Give customers access to as much of your information as possible.

Perhaps you can have terminals in your stores that will let your customers see what's in stock in the back room. Or, if you have more than one store, let them see if an item that's out of stock in one location might be available in another one. Online or in a store, give your customers the ability to check prices, search for specials, and obtain volume discount information or manufacturer's rebate availability.

Give customers access to information about their orders and accounts.

If a customer has an item on order, there's no reason why that customer should have to talk to one of your employees to find out what the status of that order is. Give your customers the ability to place special orders without the help of an associate. Let customers check their credit limits and request a larger credit line.

Let customers manage their incentive awards programs online.

One large hotel chain insists that its customers request a paper certificate in order to redeem free nights that were earned through the company's frequent guest program. This is ridiculous. If you offer something akin to incentive points, your customers should be able to redeem them online.

Let your offline customers shop online.

The Circuit City example is certainly one that you ought to study. Even if, for some reason, you don't want to actually transact business over the Web (or if you're just not yet prepared to do so), you can still allow your customers to place an order or set merchandise aside for pickup at your store.

Let your customers do their own paperwork.

If your business requires that paperwork be filled out, get your employees out of the middle and allow your customers to enter their information into your systems directly. Your customers will be happier, your associates will be freed up to pursue higher value activities, and the information in your systems will likely be far more accurate. I can't begin to tell you how many businesses have my name spelled "Columbo" in their records, even after I have spelled it out correctly ("That's C-O-L-O-M-B-O.") for the employees who were collecting my information.

Let me make a couple of final points. First, as we saw in the example of ATMs at the beginning of this chapter, one of the natural consequences of a self-service strategy is a tremendous increase in convenience for your customers. In the case of ATMs, that convenience wasn't fully realized until an information infrastructure was put in place that allowed machines to be placed in locations other than banks. As you implement self-service approaches in your business, remember that you already have an information infrastructure in place. It's called the Internet. It connects all of your business locations to each other. More importantly, it connects your customers to you no matter where they are. A client who is on a business trip halfway across the country can still have access to you over the Web and take advantage of all the self-service options you've created.

If your business gives your customer the option of self-service when it's possible, you're going to find yourself at a tremendous competitive advantage in your market. Self-service is empowering for the people who do business with you. And empowerment is a terrific strategy for capturing customers.

Remember, too, that just because customers like to do things *for* themselves doesn't necessarily mean that they like to do things *by* themselves. In fact, most people want to be a part of a community. Technology allows you to help them do just that— and to strengthen their ties to your business at the same time. In Chapter 10, I'll show you how it's done.

Create
a Community

The idea of creating a sense of community around a product of service didn't start with the Web. Over the years, lots of products have incorporated an element of "membership" or community as part of their positioning in the marketplace. American Express is a notable example of a company that's been doing this successfully for years. With American Express, you're not a "cardholder." You're a "member." A good deal of the company's marketing and advertising addresses this concept in one way or another. The idea is that you're not alone out there. The company's positioning in this regard is so comprehensive that it extends to the card itself. Each American Express card is imprinted with the date that your "membership" started.

Before the Internet, the concept of community was difficult to fully realize for most businesses. In the American Express example, even though you might have been a member, you weren't able to hang out with other "members."

You didn't go to meetings and socialize. You weren't able to call other "members" on the phone to ask their advice about anything. Heck, you couldn't even get together with other members over a beer to shoot the breeze about how great American Express did that time when you ran out of cash in Fiji. You might have belonged, but you certainly couldn't interact.

A community depends on some sort of physical connection or communications mechanism. If you are a member of a community, you probably live with or near the other members, work with them, or attend church with them. Or, at least, you get together periodically to exchange ideas about an interest you share.

Technology has changed all of that radically. It exploded the boundaries of what constituted a community when it created a communications framework that allowed people who had never met to come together and interact with each other online. They could exchange ideas, share opinions, and advise. They could argue and pontificate. And they could establish *de facto* pecking orders. In other words, they could behave substantially like traditional communities, even though the members were thousands of miles apart and were unlikely to ever get together physically or even speak to each other on the phone. In fact, many online communities evolved in ways that created exceptionally strong ties between the community and its members.

Commerce-based Communities

Although early online communities were explicitly anti-commercial, it didn't take too long for early Internet entrepreneurs (the ones who were more focused on actually doing business, not the subsequent wave of dotcom players who were more interested in their IPO than their customers and markets) to figure out that there was something important going on and that it had significant implications for capturing customers.

The results of what they created should prove useful to you as you think about building a sense of community around your own products and services.

Before we look at some examples, though, let me make one important distinction for you. Creating a community is *not* the same thing as sponsoring a chat room on your Web site. Some people would have you think that as soon as you put up a chat room, you're creating a community. That would be roughly the same as thinking that, in an offline environment, you've created a community if you've built a meeting hall. In both cases, you've merely created a structure in which a community can exist. If you really want to create a community, you've still got a lot of work to do.

Your most difficult—and important—work lies in figuring out exactly why the community ought to exist in the first place. (Driving customers to your Web site answers that question of why you should invest in creating the community. It doesn't answer the question of why any of your customers would want to bother with the community that you're creating.) You need to have an idea of what kind of value your community might be able to create for your customers.

Let's take a look at some of the more effective commerce-based communities. Then, we'll discuss how you might be able to implement these sorts of strategies in your business.

eBay

There isn't a better example anywhere of how a community can add value for customers and, as a consequence, for the business that sponsors it than eBay. In fact, it wouldn't be an exaggeration to say that eBay would probably not be possible without its online community.

If you think about it, the basic idea behind eBay is preposterous, and yet it's the most popular auction site on the Web. What sense does it make to build a business that depends on someone sending money to a stranger for merchandise that hasn't been seen? It sounds pretty implausible, doesn't it?

The answer is that it's likely that it wouldn't have worked without the ingenious online community that eBay has created. The way this community works is simple. Sellers and buyers from around the globe rate one another based on their experiences with each other in actual auctions. Feedback can be positive, negative, or neutral, and every feedback submission is allowed a brief space for comments.

A seller is rated on how closely his merchandise matches the description he gave in his listing, how responsive he was to questions that the buyer had during the course of the transaction, how quickly the merchandise was shipped at the end of the auction, and the overall quality of the transaction as perceived by the buyer. The buyer is rated on how quickly she submits payment and, again, the overall quality of the transaction, this time as perceived by the seller. Any individual on eBay can be rated as both a seller and a buyer and, in practice, is usually rated as both. Some typical, sample eBay ratings for a seller:

@   "Would most certainly buy from him again.
     Fabulous objects for sale. Bravo!!!!"

@   "Terrific seller! Fast, very friendly, a pleasure to
     deal with. Thanks a lot Eddie!"

@   "Professional transaction, pkging excellent.
     Eddie is a pleasure to deal with!!!!"

@   "Items arrived in great condition. Wonderful to
     do business with!!!!!"

(You'll notice that eBay members are big on exclamation marks!) Here are some typical, sample ratings for a buyer:

@   "Great to do business with, very prompt. Will do
     business with again."

@   "Very fast payment, good communication. Would
    definitely deal with again."

@   "Great Customer—Smooth Transaction——Fast
    Payment!"

@   "Excellent communications! Prompt payment!
    Great to do business with! Thanks!"

(For some reason that's not entirely clear to me, sellers seem
to inspire more exclamation marks than buyers.)

All of this works as well as it does because eBay has structured its system so that it's very, very difficult to "stuff the
ballot box." As a result, anyone who's reviewing the feedback
profile of a member of eBay can do so with a high degree of
confidence.

One final point: Over time, a member of the eBay community is able to earn a rating based on the cumulative total of
positive feedbacks that the member has received. The member's
rating is denoted by an icon next to his or her user name. This
means that it's not even really necessary to review the specifics of a member's profile. If you're considering doing business
with that member, you can just check his or her overall rating
at a glance. (Of course, the specifics are always there if you
care to check them out.)

Let's go back to the question I posed previously: What sense
does it make to build a business that depends on someone sending money to a stranger for merchandise that hasn't been seen?
The answer is that it makes perfect sense if you can design a
mechanism that allows buyers and sellers to have confidence
in each other and, therefore, in the transaction. The community that eBay created polices itself. This creates value for all
of the community's members and, as a result, creates tremendous value for eBay itself.

Amazon.com

Amazon does a lot of things right, and its approach to creating an online community certainly falls into that category. The idea behind what Amazon has done is extremely simple and straightforward. Anyone who wants to do so is allowed to review any of the products that Amazon sells, whether they actually purchased the product from Amazon or not. (For example, let's say that you're absolutely floored by the quality of the book that you're reading right now. You're convinced that its insights will be incredibly helpful for your business and you're impressed by the clarity of its writing. You're probably bursting at the seams to tell someone. If you wanted to, you could put the book down right now, log on to *Amazon.com,* and write a glowing review. Mind you, I'm not saying that you *should.* I'm just saying that you *could.*)

The company pays a great deal of attention to fostering its community of reviewers. For example, reviewers are allowed to post a page on Amazon's Web site identifying themselves. In addition to appearing on the individual pages of the products that are reviewed, each reviewer's submissions are compiled together in one place so that a reader can get a sense of what the reviewer's overall tastes are. Readers are able to note whether they find a particular review helpful or not. If a reviewer compiles enough "helpful" responses, he or she can be designated as a top reviewer.

It's not uncommon for popular books and CDs on Amazon to have hundreds of reviews. Even fairly obscure books and CDs will often elicit a few reviews. Each reviewer rates the product in question on a scale of from one to five stars. An average of all the reviewers' ratings is posted on the main page of a product's listing. The quality of the reviews themselves ranges from (often) erudite to (occasionally) ridiculous. Reviews are limited to 1,000 words, although most are shorter than that. There are other specific guidelines for Amazon reviews, including these stipulations (taken from Amazon's Web site):

What to include:

Your comments should focus on the book's content and context. You must also include a valid e-mail address, but you can opt not to display your e-mail address if you do not wish others to have access to it. The best reviews include not only whether you liked or disliked a book, but also why. Feel free to mention other books you consider similar and how this book rates in comparison to them. Comments that are not specific to the book will not be posted on our site.

What not to include:

Reviews for not-yet-released titles. Resist the temptation to comment on other reviews or features visible on the page. Please limit yourself to one comment per title. This information (and its position on the page) is subject to change without notice. A book review is not an appropriate place to tell us our catalog has typos in it. If you'd like to tell us about a specific problem, or want some additional information on a book, please send us e-mail at book-dept@amazon.com.

Amazon.com is proud to provide this forum for you to air your opinions on your favorite (or not-so-favorite) books. While we appreciate your time and comments, we respectfully request that you refrain from including the following in your review:

@ *Profanity, obscenities, or spiteful remarks.*

@ *Time-sensitive material (i.e., promotional tours, seminars, lectures, etc.).*

@ *Single-word reviews. We want to know why you liked or disliked the book.*

@ *Comments focusing solely on the author.*

@ *No spoilers! Please don't reveal crucial plot elements.*

@ *Personal information such as phone numbers, mailing addresses, URLs.*

@ *Availability, price, or alternative ordering/ shipping information.*

The reviewer community achieves several objectives. Obviously, an important one is that it creates significant value for the company's customers. They're able to log on to the site and get feedback, not from professional critics, but from people just like them. And this value is magnified by the quantity of reviews that Amazon generates. One or two critics might say anything, but 30 or 50 reviews represent a broad enough sampling to seriously consider when you're making a purchase.

The reviewer community also creates strong bonds between Amazon and its customers. If you were an aspiring Roger Ebert, wouldn't you gravitate strongly towards a company that gave you a forum? And wouldn't it give you an incentive to focus all of your online activities on a site that gave you that kind of visibility?

Creating Your Own Community

If we look closely at the eBay and Amazon user communities as examples, there are a few important rules for creating a successful community that we can glean.

Focus on customers.

These communities create genuine and obvious value for customers. They're explicitly not designed for the benefit of the companies that sponsor them. Instead, they're designed for their customers. The result, though, is that the companies benefit tremendously.

Don't hold the reigns too tightly.

Both eBay and Amazon have guidelines as to what is and is not permissible. Beyond those guidelines, however, the companies have adopted a relatively *laissez faire* approach. It's not unheard of, for example, for a review on Amazon to include sharp criticism of something that Amazon might have done.

This is a characteristic of other successful online communities. Dell Computer, for example, allows sometimes scathing criticism of the company on its bulletin boards. Sure, the criticism can be hard to take, but the credibility that it buys is priceless. (On the other hand, don't be too cavalier. Check with your attorney about what sorts of things you need to keep away from, and post them in your guidelines.)

Create mechanisms to prevent "stuffing the ballot box."

Both eBay and Amazon try to structure their communities in ways that prevent artificial manipulation. This is an important step in assuring the community's credibility.

Remember that the community is intrinsic to the business.

These communities are not designed for pointless chatting. They are an integral part of what each company does. They are so ingrained and add so much value that each of the companies would be substantially different without them. They're part of the business proposition.

What can you do in your own business to create community? Here are a few ideas that will go a long way towards getting you started:

@   Realize that you can create an online community for an offline business. This is one more strategy for integrating your presence on the Web with what you're doing in your stores and sales offices.

@   Start to identify ways in which your customers can create real value for each other. For example, maybe you have a local nursery. You might sponsor a community in which your customers trade tips about gardening and landscaping in your particular part of the country. Gardening is obviously a very different undertaking in Arizona than it is in Florida. If you're a Floridian, you bring some expertise to the table, but customers will only listen to what you have to say once or twice. They'll come back time after time to interact with each other.

@ Acknowledge those who participate. Amazon's Top Reviewer structure is an example of this principle in action. This principle works well even when it's confined to your online community, but it's even more effective if you can find ways to integrate it into your in-store operations. You might have a Top Contributor rating, for example, that provides some sort of small gift every month that Top Contributors can pick up in your store. You'll be astonished at the lengths to which your customers will go to reach higher and higher levels of acknowledgment.

Let me make one final point: This may be on the heretical side, but the fact of the matter is that this strategy is not for everyone. Your business model may simply not lend itself to this notion of creating a community. If that's the case, don't try to force it. You'll only wind up looking silly if you do.

So far in this book, we've looked at some extremely powerful strategies for re-creating your business and moving into the mode of capturing customers instead of selling products. In Section 3, I'm going to give you some tools for fine-tuning your efforts.

Capturing Conversations

David Weinberger

David Weinberger publishes the influential Web newsletter JOHO: The Journal of the Hyperlinked Organization *and is a technology commentator for National Public Radio's* All Things Considered. *He is also a co-author of* The Cluetrain Manifesto, *a Web phenomenon that turned into a best-selling book.*

Colombo: Tell me a little bit about the concept of markets as conversations. What do you mean when you talk about markets as conversations, and how is this concept different from the way we've looked at markets up until now?

Weinberger: What preceded this concept of markets was a view of markets as a collection of demographic sectors. We'd use the lowest common denominator so the message could be broadcast as broadly as possible, driving down the cost of marketing. Broadcasters could market to like people, if they thought of them as defined by a few salient demographic characteristics.

Once upon a time, markets were social groups made up of people who actually knew one another. Now they are social groups of people who *don't* know one another. In the sense of knowing each other in a face-to-face way, they are not really social groups at all. The Web enables—or *reenables*—people in a market to know one another and that happens through the conversation they have in various forms.

Colombo: Knowing one another on the Web might not necessarily be face-to-face, but the practical effect is the same.

Weinberger: In many ways, yes.

Colombo: For the owner of a small or medium-sized business, what are the implications of markets as conversations?

Weinberger: Attempts to use broadcast techniques for marketing may have some effect, but now that type of marketing is being done in the face of markets that are not only increasingly immune to those techniques but actually *hostile* to them. Your market now wants to talk with you and with the people who work for you. It doesn't want to be patronized with a canned message. It wants you to tell the truth.

Colombo: If you look at "conversations" on the Web, what is the appropriate role that a business should have in those conversations?

Weinberger: Generally, when companies figure out their markets, or conversations, are on the Web—and that's where the *real* information is being transferred—they want to *control* those conversations. But these are real conversations and you can't go in and manage them any more than you can go up to people at a barbecue and suddenly start broadcasting a message. You can't manage them. They're not in any sense yours. They're centered on whatever the conversation is about. Say it's golf equipment. If you're making golf equipment, the people who are talking about it are probably only secondarily interested in golf equipment. They're probably actually interested in getting better at golf. You're just not the center of their universe. You are only the center of *your* universe. And yet so many companies think that the conversation is just about them and that the customers can't wait to hear from them. In fact, the customers *can* wait to hear from them! The customers are probably out there really having a good time talking with one another. And if there is somebody in the company who can jump in and engage them like a human being and talk about golf, because he or she cares about it, that's fantastic. But if it's the PR manager who jumps in, and he or she doesn't like the stream of the conversation and wants to change it, he or she will just alienate your market.

Colombo: Should companies provide the forum for the conversation to take place? Is that an appropriate role for them to play?

Weinberger: It may be, but it's frequently not. Often there are already conversations going on, and nobody's looking to you to host it. Other times you can serve as a focal point for the few immediate users, but when you do that you have to stay well out of the way. There is a gun manufacturer who has a forum that includes occasional participation by a representative of the gun company. She jumps in when there's some factual issue she can resolve. And she doesn't do it with committee statements; she sounds like somebody who's passionate about her products. She doesn't sit there and think about how she can respond to every message and every complaint or argue every person who whines about the product.

Colombo: And she doesn't try to craft a fairy tale kind of message that says, "Gosh, everything's great."

Weinberger: Exactly. One customer, who had repeatedly complained about one of the guns overheating, mentioned that he buys secondhand ammunition to save money. To straighten him out, she didn't try to give him a cookie-cutter answer, and she didn't try to make everybody happy. She basically said, "Listen, we tell you very clearly to use a certain quality ammo. You're not doing that, so the gun is probably going to overheat." It was in her own voice, it was straightforward, it was factual, and it was human. And it hadn't been run through the lawyers or the marketing department.

Colombo: There's a shift in the balance of power between buyers and sellers, and the power is predominantly in the hands of the buyers these days. So you can't act as though things haven't changed.

Weinberger: Things have changed dramatically, and a lot of it has to do with a shift in power. Let me give you an example. There is a Volkswagen Eurovan discussion group in which one customer mentioned that he was having a problem with a fuel line leak. Sure enough, other people said, "Me, too," all of a sudden realizing that they were not alone. It turns out that there was a problem with one of the seals. The group notified Volkswagen and the proper federal agency, which ordered a recall of more than 11,000 Eurovans. This means that a conversation flipped into a political action committee.

Colombo: So you can't control it, but it doesn't make sense to ignore it either, right?

Weinberger: That's exactly right. Corporations are tied up in the notion of control. The issue is ontological. Who are you and what sort of control do you have? The very definition of a company has to do with the fact that it consists of parts that it can control. When it sees that something new is going on, its first impulse is to ask, "How we can control it?" And if we can't, then it's a threat.

We have this business of "management" identified in our minds. We can't imagine a business that's not managed. So businesses have to adjust.

Colombo: If a conversation is *not* going on, should a company to try to explicitly build a forum or create the environment for dialogue?

Weinberger: The first question you need to ask is, "Why isn't anybody talking about what I'm doing?" Say you're a regional chain of bookstores. Perhaps nobody's talking about what you're doing because the way you're doing it is commodity-based and not very interesting.

Colombo: Your real problem, then, is that you're not doing anything interesting enough to talk about?

Weinberger: Right. However, if you care about what you're doing, you can probably find other people who also care about it, and they may well want to have a conversation. The first thing you want to do is look for those conversations. If there aren't any, you can try to think of ways in which you might encourage them, perhaps by providing a place where people can ask and answer questions.

Colombo: So, starting the conversation, if you can't find one going on, is not necessarily a bad thing to do?

Weinberger: As long as it's honestly intentioned. There's a difference between doing that sort of thing, on the one hand, and setting out to do something outrageous so that you become talked about, on the other. Doing that is just the old PR gambit.

Colombo: If conversations are going on in the marketplace, does it make sense from a company's standpoint to designate people whose responsibility it is to monitor these conversations or to participate in them? In other words, should that be left to take place in an organic way or should it be orchestrated?

Weinberger: Certainly, I would want to know what's being said in discussion groups on the Web, or wherever they are, about my company. I think that would be extraordinarily useful, even though it would also sometimes be absolutely infuriating. And it's simple enough for somebody to go out and do that. But the next level of involvement is having people participate and speak, more or less, on behalf of the company. You want that to happen, but you don't want to assign it to somebody who doesn't want to do it. You want to find the people who can't wait to get into these conversations. And you want it to be people you trust will be able to participate in a way that is not overly bureaucratic.

Colombo: And you don't want to do it with a mandate to go speak the corporate language.

Weinberger: That's correct. But speaking the corporate language or, at least, conveying the official corporate message, may be useful at times. There are times when people want an official answer and they want it in the official language. They might say, "We've been trying to find out from someone at your company whether your products support such and such." You want a product manager to say, "Yes it does and here are the specs and we're committed to it." That kind of communication is important, too. Sometimes, customers want to find out officially what your company has to say. But they also want to hear from your employees. They want to hear what they have to say without the corporate filter.

Fine Tuning Your ormula for Success in a Wired World

Chapter 11

Communicating with Your Customers

A couple of revolutionary technologies are available for businesses of all sizes that want to provide a real time, highly interactive experience for their customers. I don't want to go off on a technical rant here, but I can tell you that these technologies are platform-agnostic and compatible with 100 percent of your clients' systems. In addition, their reliability far exceeds any of the IP-based alternatives that are available in the marketplace. Amazingly, I've compiled a huge amount of evidence that indicates that many of the most cutting-edge dotcom companies have no idea at all that these technologies exist or, at least, have made no attempts to implement them. So, pay attention, because when it comes to interactivity and responsiveness, this is something that can yield a tremendous competitive advantage in your marketplace.

Here are the two technologies I'm talking about:

1.   Face-to-face conversation.

2.   Telephone conversation.

Disappointed? Don't be, because when you really understand the value of these two means of communication, you'll be
in much better shape than most of your competitors. And you'll
be light years ahead of 99 percent of the dotcoms.

Don't misunderstand me. E-mail ought to be an important
part of your customer communications strategy. And there's
no question that it's going to become increasingly more important every year. (In fact, we're going to look at e-mail communications in more depth shortly.) What you need to understand,
though, is that your most effective communication will always
take place on your customers' terms, not yours. For the foreseeable future, there are going to be plenty of situations in
which your customer will prefer real time, person-to-person
communication to anything electronic.

Even a business such as Dell Computer that goes to great
lengths to position itself as an "e-business" admits that the
thousands of phone conversations it has with its customers
every day yield significant benefits. Michael Dell has stated on
several occasions that talking to customers every day has
allowed the company to glean important insights from its customers about which new technologies are hot and which are
not. As a result, Dell has been able to keep its products closely
aligned with its customers' needs. That kind of insight is not
likely to emerge from e-mail communication alone. Even then,
as Dell guides its customers to its Web site (*Dell.com*), it clearly
won't be shutting down its 800 number anytime soon.

In fact, there's some reason to believe that your 800 number and your Web site will appeal to two different groups of
customers. Guthy-Renker's CEO, Greg Renker, has looked at
this issue closely. He tested, measured, and analyzed his
company's results after promoting its Web site extensively. "We
do not appear to have any diminishment of calls into the 800

number," he explained. "We *do* have an obvious increase in people who order our brand off the Web."

The lesson is clear: Electronic communication needs to be a complement to your more traditional means of communication, not a replacement. There is a segment of your customer base that is not comfortable communicating electronically and is not going to get there in the near future. Unless you're selling technology-based products and feel that you can afford to write off this segment of the market (and, remember, even Michael Dell isn't doing that), you need a means to communicate with them on their own terms.

More important, though, is the fact that nonelectronic communication conveys qualitative information that simply doesn't come across electronically. If a customer sends an e-mail that says, "I'm interested in your Model XYZ widget," what does that mean? Is that customer looking to buy right now? Is he or she merely gathering information for a possible purchase at some undetermined time in the future? Maybe the writer of the e-mail is a high school student researching a term paper on widgets. When your communication is electronic, not only is it hard to tell, but it's also difficult to gracefully do any fact finding.

Some Problems with Nonelectronic Communication

Nonelectronic communication is basically anonymous. This is a counterintuitive point, so let me explain. Without giving it a lot of thought, most people would assume that any kind of person-to-person communication, by its very nature, cannot be anonymous. How could communication be anonymous if you're talking with someone on the phone or speaking with them face to face? And how can an e-mail message be less anonymous than person-to-person contact?

The answer is that an e-mail message always contains within itself the means to get back in touch with the person who sent it. (In other words, when someone sends you an e-mail, the sender's e-mail address is included as part of the message.) An in-person or on-the-phone contact, on the other hand, does not. Let's say that a prospective client stops into one of your sales offices to pick up some literature or stops by one of your stores to take a look at a particular product you carry. That may not be anonymous in the sense that your salesperson may have the pleasure of being able to shake the prospect's hand. But the real problem you face is that when that person has left, there's a chance that they're gone for good. If you're going to turn casual customer contacts into opportunities to capture customers, then you've got to make sure that you create mechanisms to capture the information that you'll need to stay in touch. It just doesn't make any sense to allow someone to get all the way into your office or store, or to take the time and trouble to call you on the phone, and then not make an effort to find out who that person is and get his or her name into your customer database.

Become proactive about this. It would be great if every person who contacted your business said, "Why don't you take my address and phone number in case something comes up that you feel I'd like to know about?" But you know that's just not going to happen. You need a specific set of procedures that's going to accomplish your objective. For one thing, all of your employees who are likely to come into contact with a potential customer, either in person or on the phone, need to know that efforts to capture customer information need to be made every time. They also need to be trained on exactly what you want them to do. (Remember the Radio Shack example from Chapter 5?) Obviously, you don't want employees to do anything that makes a prospect irate. If a prospect doesn't want to give your employee any information, that's okay. The point is to make sure that if you don't get the customer information, it isn't because the employee didn't try.

You'll have to come up with your own specific tactics, but here are a few ideas that you might want to tailor to your own situation and use:

@ "I'd be happy to that answer and any other questions you might have right now, but we also have an information package that is very comprehensive and I'd like to get one out to you. Could you please spell your last name?"

@ "I know you're not looking to buy right now, but we have very attractive sale pricing on this brand from time to time. It would just take a second to get you on the list of clients that we notify whenever we're going to offer special pricing."

@ "Whether you wind up with our plan or someone else's, you still might benefit from the quarterly newsletter that we publish. It's got information you can use no matter whose plan you're under."

You get the idea. The important thing is to make an effort to capture a name, mailing address, and e-mail address if you can.

Another problem with nonelectronic communication is that communications with specific customers don't always get recorded into your customer information system. An e-mail message can get archived automatically or appended to a customer's record in your customer database so that it's there for review later on. Other kinds of communication, though, can be a great deal more ephemeral.

Very casual conversations are one thing, but when one of your employees has a substantive conversation with a customer, that conversation should be recorded into your customer information system. For example, if a customer calls with a question about making a substantial change in her insurance coverage, then at least a few notes about that conversation should be recorded. As much as anything, this is a matter of habit, but it's a habit that your employees ought to be encouraged to acquire. If that customer calls up again and is fuzzy on the details of the original conversation, it's very helpful if they're handy. Also, if the customer calls back and the employee who originally handled the call is not available, it's impressive if another employee has the ability to pick right up where the last conversation left off without the customer having to explain everything again. From a sales and marketing standpoint, this enhances the confidence that a customer has in your organization significantly.

E-mail to the Rescue

Another problem with nonelectronic communications is that there are times when it isn't convenient for your prospect or customer to actually come into your business or call you on the phone. This is the case, for example, when a customer has a question at three in the morning and wants to get it of his chest before he gets back to *Dragnet* reruns on Nick at Night. It's also true that there will be a significant group of customers who, for one reason or another, simply prefer to communicate via e-mail. Whatever the reason, as I said earlier, e-mail is an important communications conduit today and will inevitably become even more important in years to come. Because that's the case, let's turn our attention now to the principles you're going to need to know if you want to communicate effectively with e-mail.

Because e-mail is an increasingly important medium for communicating with your customers, the quality of your e-mail communication will influence your customer's perception of your company. It's therefore worth paying attention to some of these fundamental rules. Let me give you an analogy: Remember that afternoon last year when you ordered the spinach quiche for lunch? You spent the afternoon meeting with clients, then stopped in a restroom before leaving for home and discovered you had some green stuff lodged between your teeth. All afternoon, you looked like an idiot, but no one bothered to tell you.

You could have a similar situation on your hands when it comes to e-mail. Lots of businesses that wouldn't dream of allowing a less-than-professional letter go out to a client are somehow clueless when it comes to electronic communication. Part of the problem is that e-mail has an etiquette all its own. If you ignore the (previously) unwritten rules, you may as well be walking around with green stuff in your teeth. Here are my tips for keeping your electronic image up to par:

Use a meaningful subject line.

When a busy executive can't figure out what an e-mail message is about from the subject (particularly if the sender is not familiar), the message usually gets ignored or deleted. Also, don't get cute. If your subject line is "Important Message," it had better really be important, or your e-mails might never be read again.

Be concise.

Shakespeare observed, "Brevity is the soul of wit." In a business environment that runs on Internet time, it is also the essence of effective communication. Your client doesn't have the time to wade through the equivalent of a novel. Send her the Cliffs Notes version instead.

Stick to plain text.

Sure, it would be great to send out magnificently formatted messages. Unfortunately, some mail systems choke on formatted messages, and you have no idea what kind of e-mail system your reader has. Your beautiful message may very well wind up a disjointed mess. Plain text is the lowest common denominator in the world of e-mail. Your message may not look quite as pretty as you want, but it won't look worse than it did when you sent it.

Pay attention to grammar, spelling, and punctuation.

I know that it's fashionable among dotcom denizens to disregard everything they ever learned in English class, but your client may not yet have risen to that same level of "cool." Grammar and punctuation make your message more easily understood. Virtually every e-mail program today has a spellchecker; use it.

Resist the temptation to circulate jokes.

You may think the one about the horse walking into the bar is hysterical, but one or two of your customers will think it's stupid. And the number of people who will think it enhances your professionalism will be zero.

Avoid large attachments.

If all of your customers had a high-speed Internet connection, this would not be an issue. But your most important client might just be checking her e-mail on a dial-up line in a hotel room. She won't appreciate your choking up her system with a file that takes 15 minutes to download. If you can, use a hyperlink to a Web location that has the same information. If that's not possible, at least send a heads-up before transmitting something that's particularly large.

Think before you send.

Once you hit the "Send" button, your message is probably gone for good. Never send an e-mail when you're angry or irritated. Instead, store it in your Outbox or Unsent mail box until you're certain that you're not going to regret what you said.

Be as responsive as you'd be in any other communications medium.

There's no excuse for not replying to a customer's e-mail on a timely basis. You wouldn't ignore a customer who stopped by your sales office to ask a question. You wouldn't deliberately abandon a customer on the phone who was on hold. For the same reasons, make sure that you're timely in your responses to customer or prospect communications by e-mail. In fact, when you reply promptly, it sends a clear and powerful message about what kind of business you really are.

Ultimately, your most effective medium for communicating with a particular customer is going to be the medium that your customer prefers. Your job, then, is to make sure that your business is structured to handle all kinds of customer communications effectively. Create a structure that systematizes your nonelectronic interactions, but personalizes your electronic communications. It will take some discipline and some work, but if your customer communications aren't working properly, chances are that none of the rest of your sales and marketing effort will be, either.

Communicating is great, but wouldn't it be terrific if you could create a situation where your clients just kept coming back, over and over again, for more of what you're selling? Of course it would. In Chapter 12, I'll offer strategies for making that happen.

Building Customer Loyalty Into Your Business Structure

I n 1999, according to the FAA, there were more than 1,000 cases of assault by passengers on airline employees. I don't know what business you're in, but my guess is that you probably aren't in a business that regularly infuriates its customers to the point of physical hostility. Yet the airline industry has created a strategy for promoting brand loyalty that's incredibly effective. It works in spite of an overall level of service so poor that no one is surprised by passengers regularly losing their tempers in a big way.

If you're heading up your company's sales and marketing efforts, then, here's the question you ought to be asking yourself: If a customer loyalty strategy exists that's so effective it works even in the airline industry, how well would it possibly work in a business such as mine, an industry that tries to take good care of its customers? The answer is that it can work incredibly well if you take the time to adopt it to fit your particular situation. The strategy I'm referring to, of course, is the frequent flier program.

The basic premise is simple: A customer earns points or miles for flying on a particular airline. That sort of basic incentive is nothing new. It's a variation of Green Stamps, an incentive program that supermarkets used extensively years ago. The special wrinkle that frequent flier programs have added is that the value of the program escalates dramatically the more you use it. Each airline has levels of membership that are attained when a certain number of miles are flown in a calendar year. Each level, in turn, has its own set of perks, including easier and easier access to the highly coveted First Class upgrade.

Airlines segment their customers according to value. More valuable customers get treated differently than less valuable customers. It is this principle of *escalating value* that we're going to examine as we explore ways to build incentives into your business that will keep your customers coming back for more. The resulting customer loyalty is what capturing customers is all about.

And, if you think about it, it really doesn't make much sense to *not* build this principle into your overall marketing approach. As we've seen already, repeat customers are almost always more profitable to you than new customers. There are a number of ways to encourage repeat business (we've talked about several of them already), but none of them is more powerful than this. Done properly, your customers will go out of their way to do business with you.

A colleague of mine is a great example of this. As do most frequent fliers, she pays close attention to her status. She always knows exactly where she stands and what she needs to do to reach the next level of membership. Last December, she realized that she needed two more travel segments to reach the highest membership level that her airline offered. When she realized that she didn't have any more client engagements on the books, she booked a visit to a friend's place in a nearby city just so she could get the extra segments she needed.

Obviously, the concept of customer loyalty programs is not a new one. What's new is the fact that technology has put this type of approach well within the reach of small and medium-sized businesses that could not have undertaken it—except in the most rudimentary way—before. And the Internet has provided a mechanism that allows you to start with the basic concepts of escalating value and escalating incentives and then use the Web to tie your customers to you even more closely. In other words, you're using the Web to create "electronic incentives." (These are sometimes generically referred to as "e-centives," but I'm avoiding that term here in order to not cause any confusion with a dotcom company of the same name.)

Lots of Variations on a Theme

One of the things that makes this principle of escalating value so powerful is your ability to tailor it to fit your specific circumstances. In fact, there are a number of different approaches to building escalating value into your business structure. Your approach will reflect your specific objectives. Are you trying to get customers to shop more frequently? Purchase more frequently? Are you trying to stave off inroads by competitors? Whatever you're trying to accomplish in terms of customer loyalty, there are ways to do it.

Let's take a look at a few of the options you can choose from when you're crafting a customer loyalty program. These are not mutually exclusive strategies. Rather, they represent various elements that you can pick and choose from—like a buffet—and blend into your own unique approach to creating customer loyalty:

Value from Aggregated Purchases

This is probably the most common approach, although there are a number of variations that you can use to make it interesting. It is the basic approach that we discussed earlier that is used by the airlines with much success. The underlying idea is that a customer's benefits increase as his or her aggregate purchases accumulate over a specified period of time.

The most unimaginative variation on this theme (not completely ineffective, just unimaginative) is an earned discount based on total sales volume. A discount program awards your larger customers and encourages all of your customers to place as much of their business as possible with your company. There are a number of problems with this approach, not the least of which is that it distills the terms of your relationship with your customer down to price, which is basically a zero sum game. It doesn't create loyalty beyond a competitor's ability to meet the price that your customer has earned at his or her particular discount level.

Another lackluster variation of this approach is to reward cumulative purchases. Businesses that take this tact will, for example, offer a "free" item after some specified number of the same item has been purchased. In effect, this is the same thing as a volume discount, with all of the same drawbacks. It offers the additional drawback, however, of dropping the customer back to "ground zero" after he's gotten his freebie. For example, if you offer a free round of golf after the customer has paid for nine rounds, you're basically offering a 10-percent discount on 10 rounds. But once your client has used his free round, he's back to his regular price and has no immediate incentive to continue to play at your course.

A more plausible approach is to look for ways to create value that is based on service and other intangibles. In effect, what you'd want to do is create an equivalent to the airlines' First

Class upgrade. Could you offer an upgraded delivery option? Or maybe some kind of Express Service option?

It's also worth your time and effort to try to create levels of value that are difficult for a competitor to duplicate. Is there something you could offer to elite level customers that your competitors couldn't (or wouldn't) match? For example, American Express offers its Gold Card members the option to buy special tickets at various theater and entertainment events during the course of the year. Could you create an event for your special customers? Maybe a "members only" workshop or seminar featuring a popular speaker for your top-level business clients?

Value from Customer Information

As you do business with your clients over time, you learn more and more about their needs and preferences. If you can translate that increasing amount of knowledge into tangible value for your customer, then you've got a winning customer loyalty formula.

This value is predicated on a couple of things. First of all, it assumes that information about your customer is being accumulated into a customer information system. Then, it assumes that you're analyzing the accumulated information to search for patterns and associations that create value. The bad news is that these are not necessarily simple undertakings. The good news is that they can provide radical differentiation for your business.

In Chapter 5, we discussed one example of this principle when we looked at *Amazon.com*'s book recommendation service. The basic approach behind Amazon's system is a proprietary software engine that looks at what books a particular customer has purchased recently, finds other customers who purchased those same books, then checks to see what books those customers purchased and recommends them to the original customer. As a result, the more you shop with Amazon, the more valuable they potentially are to you. *That* is the hallmark of success for extracting value from a customer information and translating that value into customer loyalty. That is a real electronic incentive.

As one software company's ad puts it, "Success comes from anticipating your customers' needs before they do." This is not easy, but don't be put off by the challenge. Amazon has invested in a sophisticated and extremely expensive system, but you don't necessarily have to. A reasonably robust customer information system can deliver much of the same information at a fraction of the cost.

Keep one other thing in mind: If you're going to use information in this way to create customer loyalty, it's not necessary for your systems to be as good as Amazon's. It's only necessary for them to be better than any of your competitor's. And given the fact that it's unlikely that any of your competitors are going to undertake anything remotely like this, chances are that you're going to be in pretty good shape.

Survey Value

It's possible to create value that is similar to customer information value without actually having to accumulate large amounts of customer information over time. You can do this by giving a customer the opportunity to "manually" provide you with equivalent information through a ratings system. *Netflix.com,* a company that rents DVDs over the Internet, is a good example of this approach.

On the Netflix Web site, a customer is given the opportunity to rate movies that she's seen on a scale of one to five stars. The customer can rate as many movies as she chooses. Then, based on the ratings, the Netflix system provides customized movie recommendations.

Altough this particular example uses a ratings system, the same principle can be applied in other ways. You might give your prospect an opportunity to take a survey and then, based on the survey results, you could provide some recommendations. You could structure your system similar to Netfix's if you wanted, so that a minimum number of questions would yield certain results, but answering more questions would refine your recommendations even further.

Contests

This is one of the most reliable mechanisms ever designed to keep customers coming back. It's an approach that works in industry after industry and one that has worked dependably time after time. This basic idea is that each visit to your location or your Web site gives your customer an entry into a contest. The more the customer is entered, the better his chances of winning are.

There are several advantages to this approach. One is that there is a certain entertainment value to a contest. People enjoy being entered and they enjoy hearing the results, even when they themselves are not the winners. (Obviously, though, winning is more fun!) An important point to remember, then, is to make certain that you publicize your results, in your store or sales office and on your Web site.

Another attractive aspect of contest-based loyalty programs is that you can expand the program dramatically without a proportionate increase in your cost. Let's say that you own a beauty salon and you've created a customer loyalty program that gives your top customers a free bottle of shampoo with every other haircut. If you double the enrollment in your program, you double its potential cost to you. You're on the hook for twice as many bottles of shampoo. On the other hand, let's say you decide to run a weekly contest to give away a free shampoo, haircut, and style. If you get 20 entries in your contest, you're on the hook for what it costs you to provide one free set of services. But if you get 50 entries, or even 100, your cost doesn't change. You've extended the marketing impact of your program significantly for approximately the same amount of money.

One last comment about contests. They're extremely effective, but they also represent an easy way to get blindsided by legal problems that you never anticipated or considered. Talk to your attorney before undertaking anything beyond the simplest and most straightforward contest programs.

Referrals

This is probably the most effective, yet most underutilized customer loyalty technique that exists. I'm going to skip over what would otherwise be an extended discussion of the underlying psychological principles that are at work here. Instead, I'm going to get right to the bottom line: Customers who refer other customers to your business will be demonstrably more loyal (and more profitable) than customers who don't refer. This means that you can increase the loyalty and profitability of existing customers by getting them to refer more business to you. And, by the way, you'll also be getting new customers in the process. I'll come back to the new customer aspect of this approach, but let's look at this business of referrals first.

The overwhelming majority of businesses—this applies to businesses that sell to consumers as well as businesses that sell to other businesses—never ask a client or customer for a referral. I can understand, if not exactly condone, the reluctance of business owners and their salespeople to come right out and ask for a referral. But the situation is even worse than that. Almost as many businesses don't even provide a mechanism for customers who want to give a referral. There's just no defensible reason for that kind of oversight.

Certainly, your Web site is a great place to build in this kind of capability. You can simply have your customer fill in a colleague's e-mail address on a form. The click of a mouse would trigger an e-mail message that would appear to come from your customer's e-mail address containing a brief, prewritten greeting (which your customer could edit if he or she wanted to) and a link to your Web site. It would also trigger a flag in your customer information system that would send an e-mail to your customer, thanking him for the referral. (If you wanted to *really* knock his socks off, you could have the system alert the sales clerk to deliver a personal thank you the next time your customer came into your store!)

As I mentioned, there's a double payoff in this one. The first is that the referring customer is likely to become committed and more profitable to you as a result of a principle that psychologists refer to as *commitment and consistency*. The second payoff is that you get a new customer who, because he came to you as the result of a referral, is much more likely to refer even more customers to you. The whole process, at its best, turns into a happily repeating cycle.

The Incentive

Here's something that's very counterintuitive but, at the same time, very important for you to know: The objective value of whatever incentives you choose to offer in a customer loyalty program have no relationship to the perceived value to your customer.

In other words, you can build incentives into your customer loyalty program that have a high perceived value to your customers, but that don't cost you very much. We already discussed one example of this when we looked at contest incentives. There are others, though, that might be more suited to your business. Different service levels, for example, typically do not cost much to implement but come with a high perceived value. (It's hard to overstate the value that customers place on even the smallest symbols of status.)

The key to enhancing the perceived value of an incentive lies in a principle that is one of the oldest adages in sales: Sell the sizzle. Going back to the airline example for a moment, one of the perks of elite membership at most airlines is that you are allowed to use a special line for check-in. As a practical matter, the wait at the regular line is sometimes less than it is at the elite members' line. But do you think that many elite members walk over to the other line to get checked in more quickly? Of course not.

Tying it all Together

Technology is obviously a key to customer loyalty programs when it comes to their administration. But don't overlook the fact that customer loyalty programs are a great vehicle for driving your customers to your Web site. If your program is positioned properly, your customers will visit your site regularly to check on their status within the program or to perform any administrative functions related to your program. For example, if they can redeem points for merchandise, you'd want to drive them to your site to do that.

Contests are another example of how a loyalty program can drive Web traffic. In the case of a contest, you could send an e-mail to registered customers that says, "We've got another monthly winner. Click here to visit our Web site to see if it's you!" This is an opportunity to step up the frequency of your proactive contacts with your registered customers without being intrusive. Note that you're not e-mailing customers with the name of the winner. You're e-mailing them to drive them to your Web site.

One last point about tying everything together with the Web: Your Web site and your customer information site should be working hand in hand. The people in your store or sales office should be utilizing the same data that your customers see on the Web. And all of your customers' activities—on the Web, in the store, in your sales office, or with your salesperson in the field—should be posted to that same database. The Web is the glue that ties it all together.

The number of ways that you can implement a customer loyalty program is almost endless. But if you think it through and design a program that represents a high perceived value to your customer, the results are always the same: increased sales, enhanced profitability, and a better outcome when it comes to capturing customers.

This is only one instance where the use of technology to drive sales and marketing can yield terrific results, but it's also an example of an issue that is increasingly of concern to your customers. As a result, it ought to be of increasing concern to you, too. I'm referring to the issues of privacy and permissions. That's the topic of Chapter 13.

Respecting Privacy and Getting Permission

I gave a lot of thought to the title of this book. It was important to me to have the title reflect the basic spirit of the message I'm trying to convey, and I think *Capturing Customers.com* does a pretty good job of that. To get this chapter started, though, let me share with you some of the titles that I rejected as unsuitable:

@ Taking Advantage of Customers.com

@ Exploiting Customers.com

@ Fooling Customers.com

@ Selling Out Your Customers.com

There might have been a few others, but you get the idea. The message of this book is that it is in your best interest as a businessperson to forge long-term, sustainable relationships with your customers. There are other ways of doing business, but they are not part of the message here. If your reaction to this chapter is that the principles I've outlined here leave some money on the table in the short run, you're probably right. There are certainly some tactics that I recommend against in this chapter that might squeeze some extra money out of your customer base in the short term. They're just not a part of my marketing philosophy.

Your long-term relationship with your customers is your company's most valuable asset. Unless you're planning to visit bankruptcy court some time in the near future, anything you do that threatens to undermine that relationship just doesn't make sense. Thankfully, in most areas of your business, it's unlikely that you'll make a major mistake without at least being aware that you're operating in questionable territory. Online, however, it's possible to inadvertently alienate a large segment of your customer base because you're not familiar with the cultural attitudes and sensibilities that customers bring to the Web. My objective in this chapter is to help you avoid any unintentional missteps.

Perception is Reality

For the most part, doing business on the Web is at least as secure as anywhere else. Web security is a great deal like airline safety. Relative to the overall volume of business, problems are extremely rare. But when they occur, they can be devastating, and they almost always receive a great deal of attention and scrutiny. For example, in 1999, one dotcom Web site was invaded by crackers who downloaded tens of thousands of credit card records, then ineptly attempted to blackmail the site for their safe return. The incident stayed in the news for days, in spite of the fact that no one lost a dime.

From a marketing standpoint, though, as long as you've implemented the standard security safeguards, the relative safety of online transaction is not your primary concern. (Standard safeguards would include conducting your transactions from a secure area of your Web site. Your Webmaster or Web hosting company can easily take care of this for you.) What's more important is the perception of your customers. Whether your customers are safe or not doesn't matter if they don't feel that they're safe. Your response to customer's security concerns should include a thorough explanation of why transactions on your site are safe. Here's how Barnes & Noble does it on its Web site:

Our Guarantee

Shopping with Barnes & Noble.com is absolutely safe — you never have to worry about credit-card safety when you are shopping at our site. We guarantee that each purchase you make is protected and safe. If fraudulent charges are ever made, you will not have to pay for them. See guarantee details below.

How We Make Shopping Safe

We use the latest encryption technology to keep your personal information safe. All your ordering information — including your name, address, and credit card number — is encrypted using a secure server for maximum security. Your credit card and billing information cannot be read as it travels to our ordering system. To ensure that your information is even more secure, once we receive your credit card information, we store it on a server that isn't accessible from the Internet.

Guarantee Details

In general, under federal law, you will not be liable for more than $50 of fraudulent charges. In the unlikely event that you are subject to fraudulent charges, remember to first notify your credit card provider in accordance with its reporting rules and procedures. If, for whatever reason, you are held responsible for this amount, Barnes & Noble.com will cover the entire liability for you, up to $50, as long as the unauthorized use of your credit card resulted through no fault of your own from purchases made from Barnes & Noble.com while using our secure server.

That's pretty clear and straightforward, and it covers all the bases.

Don't assume that your customers know about their rights as a buyer or protections that exist in the law. If you're transacting business on your Web site, it only makes sense for you to spell these things out clearly and in plain English. (If your explanation sounds as though it was written by your attorney, it will make things worse, not better.) If you are open and clear about your security policies and design them to protect your customers' interests, you'll be in pretty good shape and able to turn your attention to a matter that's more pressing in the minds of your customers than your site's security.

What's More Important than Security?

Although it's true that your site's security procedures are important to some of your customers, your privacy policies and procedures are a much more likely place for you to get into trouble. Practices that are relatively commonplace in other sales and marketing circumstances can drive your online customers into an irate frenzy. You can argue all you want about how little sense it makes for them to get so incensed about something that you believe is relatively innocuous, but you'd be wasting your time and energy. It's a lot easier, and a great deal more productive, to just make sure that your online marketing conforms to the standards of the online community.

Those standards are pretty uncomplicated. Your customers on the Web want control over their information. Don't do anything that invades or compromises the privacy of your customers without letting them know about it and giving them the opportunity to opt out if they want. It is translating those apparently simple principles into practical guidelines that can be challenging.

The downside for not doing so can be significant. First of all, as I mentioned earlier, word of mouth on the Web is more significant than it is elsewhere. If a customer feels that you've done something that is unacceptable (or even questionable), it's not uncommon for him to create an e-mail saying so and send it to everyone in his address book. From there—if it's interesting, outrageous, or otherwise noteworthy—it can get forwarded over and over again until you've got a *real* public relations problem.

Also, it's not uncommon for privacy violations to make the news. Your particular transgression might not get on the radar screen at *The New York Times*, but it very well might make it into the business section of your local paper. And that's as far as it needs to get, when you think about it, to cause you a big problem.

As I just mentioned, activities that are perceived as serious transgressions on the Web might very well be commonplace elsewhere. For example, many businesses share, trade, or sell their customer lists to other businesses or to mailing list vendors. The customer is almost never asked for permission to use his or her name. This practice is by no means limited to shady outfits or fly-by-night operations. The truth is that some of the most trusted and familiar names in American business engage in this practice regularly. It is a well-established, lucrative part of their business model, and no one thinks twice about it.

That same practice on the Web, though, can be perceived to be a major breach of privacy and confidentiality. Does it make sense that sharing an e-mail address would provoke more ire than sharing your home address? Not at all—but that's beside the point. The point is that this is an issue that customers care about and that's all there is to it.

Does this mean that you can never share your customer list? Not at all. It just means that you shouldn't ever do so without letting your customers know that it's possible and giving them an opportunity to opt out if they so choose. In a way, it would be accurate to say that, strictly speaking, the issue is more one of control than privacy. Either way, it's clearly in your best interest to accommodate the prevailing sentiment of the marketplace.

If this is an issue that concerns you as a marketer—and it should—or if it is something that you're thinking about for the first time, you should know about an organization called TRUSTe. This organization defines itself as "an independent, nonprofit privacy initiative dedicated to building users' trust and confidence on the Internet and accelerating growth of the Internet industry." In effect, it performs the same function relative to Web site privacy that UL Labs performs relative to product safety. Think of it as a *Good Housekeeping* Seal of Approval that a Web site can get for its privacy policies.

Becoming a TRUSTe licensee, which entitles you to display the organization's "trustmark" on your Web site, is affordable for any size business and certainly makes a tangible statement to your customers about the seriousness of your concern for their privacy. Even if you don't become a part of the program, though, the TRUSTe Web site (*Truste.com*) is worth checking out. It will give you a fairly comprehensive look at the issue of customer privacy. For example, it provides a model privacy statement that you can modify for your own site. Here are some excerpts from that statement (along with a few comments and observations from me). These passages should suggest some of the specific issues you ought to be addressing for your customers:

Information Collection and Use

Company X is the sole owner of the information collected on this site. We will not sell, share, or rent this information to others in ways different from what is disclosed in this statement. Company X collects information from our users at several different points on our Web site.

What you're saying is that you're going to be collecting information, but that no other business or individual will have access to that information except under specific circumstances that you'll describe in advance to your customer. This is the foundation of the agreement that you make with your customer about his or her privacy.

Registration

In order to use this Web site, a user must first complete the registration form. During registration a user is required to give their contact information (such as name and e-mail address). This information is used to contact the user about the services on our site for which they have expressed interest. It is optional for the user to provide demographic information (such as income level and gender), and unique identifiers (such as social security number), but encouraged so we can provide a more personalized experience on our site.

There may be some information that you'd like, as a marketer, in order to tailor your site to his or her specific needs or to provide targeted marketing offers. Here, you let the customer know why you're asking these apparently intrusive question and you're giving the customer the option to not answer them.

As an aside, it's my personal belief that it's probably never a good idea to ask for a Social Security number; doing so can be seen as invasive or intrusive. There are lots of other identifiers you can use that will accomplish the same thing.

Order

We request information from the user on our order form. Here a user must provide contact information (such as name and shipping address) and financial information (such as credit card number, expiration date). This information is used for billing purposes and to fill customer's orders. If we have trouble processing an order, this contact information is used to get in touch with the user.

Cookies

A cookie is a piece of data stored on the user's hard drive containing information about the user. Usage of a cookie is in no way linked to any personally identifiable information while on our site. Once the user closes their browser, the cookie simply terminates. For instance, by setting a cookie on our site, the user would not have to log in a password more than once, thereby saving time while on our site. If a user rejects the cookie, he or she may still use our site. The only drawback to this is that the user will be limited in some areas of our site. For example, the user will not be able to participate in any of our Sweepstakes, Contests, or monthly Drawings that take place. Cookies can also enable us to track and target the interests of our users to enhance the experience on our site.

Some of our business partners use cookies on our site (for example, advertisers). However, we have no access to or control over these cookies.

Cookies are not necessarily evil. In fact, they can make your site a great deal easier and more functional for your customer. The issues that concern most users are disclosure and control. This part of your privacy statement lets the user know what your site might do to his or her computer, why that might happen, and what the user's options are.

Log Files

We use IP addresses to analyze trends, administer the site, track user's movement, and gather broad demographic information for aggregate use. IP addresses are not linked to personally identifiable information.

This is pretty self-explanatory. If you're going to explain what cookies are, though, it might also be a good idea to explain what IP addresses are.

Sharing

We will share aggregated demographic information with our partners and advertisers. This is not linked to any personal information that can identify any individual person.

We use an outside shipping company to ship orders, and a credit card processing company to bill users for goods and services. These companies do not retain, share, store, or use personally identifiable information for any secondary purposes.

We partner with another party to provide specific services. When the user signs up for these services, we will share names, or other contact information that is necessary for the third party to provide these services.

These parties are not allowed to use personally identifiable information except for the purpose of providing these services.

Links

This Web site contains links to other sites. Please be aware that we [COMPANY X] are not responsible for the privacy practices of such other sites. We encourage our users to be aware when they leave our site and to read the privacy statements of each and every Web site that collects personally identifiable information. This privacy statement applies solely to information collected by this Web site.

Chances are that your site links to one or more other sites. You're letting your customer know that those other sites might not necessarily share your concern for privacy issues.

Surveys and Contests

From time-to-time our site requests information from users via surveys or contests. Participation in these surveys or contests is completely voluntary, and the user therefore has a choice whether or not to disclose this information.

Information requested may include contact information (such as name and shipping address) and demographic information (such as zip code, age level). Contact information will be used to notify the winners and award prizes. Survey information will be used for purposes of monitoring or improving the use and satisfaction of this site.

Supplementation of Information

In order for this Web site to properly fulfill its obligation to our customers, it is necessary for us to supplement the information we receive with information from third party sources.

For example, to determine if our customers qualify for one of our credit cards, we use their name and social security number to request a credit report. Once we determine a user's creditworthiness, this document is destroyed.

OR

In order for this Web site to enhance its ability to tailor the site to an individual's preference, we combine information about the purchasing habits of users with similar information from our partners, Company Y and Company Z, to create a personalized user profile. When a user makes a purchase from either of these two companies, the companies collect and share that purchase information with us so we can tailor the site to our users' preferences.

Special Offers

We send all new members a welcoming e-mail to verify password and username. Established members will occasionally receive information on products, services, special deals, and a newsletter. Out of respect for the privacy of our users we present the option to not receive these types of communications. Please see our choice and opt-out below.

Site and Service Updates

We also send the user site and service announcement updates. Members are not able to unsubscribe from service announcements, which contain important information about the service. We communicate with the user to provide requested services and in regards to issues relating to their account via e-mail or phone.

Correction/Updating Personal Information

If a user's personally identifiable information changes (such as your zip code), or if a user no longer desires our service, we will endeavor to provide a way to correct, update or remove that user's personal data provided to us. This can usually be done at the member information page or by e-mailing our customer support.

Some sites may also provide telephone or postal mail options for updating or correcting personal information.

This is an important policy that works to your customers' benefit as well as yours. It is a practical demonstration of the principle that your customers "own" their information. For your part, your customers will keep their information current so that you're not trying to work with out-of-date information.

Choice/Opt-out

Our users are given the opportunity to opt out of having their information used for purposes not directly related to our site at the point where we ask for the information. For example, our order form has an opt out mechanism so users who buy a product from us, but don't want any marketing material, can keep their e-mail address off of our lists.

Users who no longer wish to receive our newsletter or promotional materials from our partners may opt out of receiving these communications by replying to unsubscribe in the subject line in the e-mail or e-mail us at support@thiswebsite.com.

Some sites are able to offer opt-out mechanisms on member information pages and also supply a telephone or postal option as a way to opt out.

Users of our site are always notified when their information is being collected by any outside parties. We do this so our users can make an informed choice as to whether they should proceed with services that require an outside party, or not.

As I mentioned earlier, a no-nonsense privacy policy does not mean that you can never share information or use it for explicitly commercial purposes. It just means that you need to inform your customers of what you're doing and allow them to opt out if they so choose. Look at it this way: The customers who don't opt out will likely be more responsive than an average customer. After the opt outs, you'll be left with a pretty good list.

Notification of Changes

If we decide to change our privacy policy, we will post those changes on our homepage so our users are always aware of what information we collect, how we use it, and under circumstances, if any, we disclose it. If at any point we decide to use personally identifiable information in a manner different from that stated at the time it was collected, we will notify users by way of an e-mail. Users will have a choice as to whether or not we use their information in this different manner. We will use information in accordance with the privacy policy under which the information was collected.

@ @ @

Of course, it's not necessary for you to adhere to this model exactly. The important thing is for you to give these issues the thought and attention they deserve, then craft a policy that addresses the concerns of your customers while still meeting your needs as a businessperson. Understand that this is not just the right way to do business based on some abstract principle of doing the proper thing. It's the right way to do business based on your self-interest as a businessperson who wants to make long term profits in the marketplace by capturing customers.

Capturing Conversations

Seth Godin

Seth Godin is the author of several best-selling books about marketing in a wired environment, including Permission Marketing *and* Unleashing the Ideavirus, *his latest book.*

Colombo: Let me play devil's advocate. If you can buy a CD-ROM for $50 that has 10 bizillion e-mail addresses, and it costs you virtually nothing to use it, why not just drop the bomb? What's the argument for a small-business person with a constrained budget against doing that?

Godin: Because what you will create is not brand equity or brand loyalty, but brand *rage*. And the idea that you can interrupt people by e-mail, poking them in a place they don't want to be poked, and believe that there are going to be no implications for your brand or businesses—when it's been proven over and over again that there are—is ridiculous. There's not one company in the Fortune 1000 that is successfully spamming people and making money at it. Because if people know where to find you, they *will* find you and do whatever they can to hurt your brand.

Colombo: Even if you're a small-business person?

Godin: A small-business person who wants to be anonymous, who wants to go steal a couple of minutes from every single one of a million people and can hide behind anonymity, they might make a few bucks. That's why there are spammers out there. But they're surely not going to be proud of it, and they're certainly not going to be able to build any kind of long-term business.

Colombo: It's the long-term ramifications that really argue against unsolicited e-mail, then.

Godin: It's a similar model to if you decide to make a career out of stealing 10 cents worth of bubble gum every time you go to the store. You're probably not going end up in prison, but it takes a long time to make a lot of money and it's nothing you'd want to tell your kids about.

Colombo: That makes a lot of sense. Let me ask you about this concept of interrupting a potential customer with a marketing message. Is there a different dynamic that comes into play when you're talking about somebody's electronic Inbox versus their TV set or their regular mailbox?

Godin: Absolutely. There's a compact that was made when you bought a TV. The deal was, you get your TV programming for free and in exchange we get to interrupt you with ads. When the telephone was invented, for 50 years the deal was that anyone who calls you is someone you want to talk to. In the 1960s, they started calling people at home during dinner. People could have said, "Stop this," and it would have gone away. But companies got away with it, so it grew and grew and grew. Well, when they started spamming people 12 years ago in e-mail, consumers had wised up. They said, "Don't do this! Stop now!" So the deal is different.

Colombo: Tell me about the concept of permission.

Godin: For 100 years the way mass marketing worked was very straightforward. Mass marketing was about using socially acceptable ways of interrupting strangers—mass marketing advertising—and doing it often enough that if you interrupted enough people, you made money doing it. And that's how Proctor & Gamble grew to $2.2 billion in advertising expenditures in 1999 alone. Because what it does is, every time it runs an ad for Wisk, it makes more money than the ad costs to run. So, that's a good idea. What permission is about is this: 1) Consumers now have choices. There are not three TV networks; there are 100. There aren't 10 Web sites; there are 40 million. So consumers don't have to listen to your ads anymore; 2) There's way more clutter, way more advertising than there ever was; and 3) Everything is really good, so consumers don't need to pay attention to advertising the way they used to. And when you add those three things together, what you get is the fact that advertising to people who don't want to hear from you is a bad idea. And what permission is about is, very simply, delivering anticipated, personal, and relevant advertising to people who want to get it.

Colombo: Now, when you talk about a targeted, personalized message—

Godin: Wait a second. I didn't say "targeted," and I didn't use the word "personalized." I said "personal." There's a difference.

Colombo: What's the difference between "personal" and "personalized"?

Godin: "Personalized" implies that you did something to scam people into believing that you were doing it just for them. "Targeted" is a word that usually is associated with a gun. You aim a gun at a target, so this infers a sort of inappropriate aggression in pursuit of a customer. Both of those words represent old marketing thinking. Both of them are about the fact that the marketer is in charge, he can "target" who he wants, he can "personalize" the note. That's not what this is. This is people raising their hands and saying, "I am looking forward to hearing from you about a message that is relevant to me and personal." Now, you may have to personalize the message to make it personal, but it's all about they're hearing it from the user's point of view, not the marketer's point of view.

Colombo: How do you get people to want to get this message?

Godin: The way you used to do it, which still works great, is through acceptable media, such as TV and magazines and classifieds, where people are eager to hear mass marketing messages. You say, "If you call us or write to us or raise your hand in some other way, we will give you this. We will give you information, we will give you a chance to win a prize, we will give you a coupon, we will give you a free consultation, we will clean your carpets." That's what help wanted ads are. They don't say, "We're giving you this job." Help wanted ads say, "If you call us, we will read your resume." And once that person raises his or her hand, you can have a permission-based relationship.

The best way to create permission-based relationships is to get your customers to tell their friends. It says that people marketing to each other are dramatically more effective than marketers marketing to people.

Colombo: Do these principles work differently when they're applied by the small-business person than when they're applied by larger businesses?

Godin: There's a tremendous advantage for the small-business person. What happens is, the large guys want to automate the thing. They want to bring in consultants; they want to do CRM. A small-business person is going to do it by hand. And doing it by hand is *exactly* the right way to start.

Colombo: And, going back to a point you made earlier, you're at a point as a small business where it's not "personalized." It is "personal," period.

Godin: Right. The problem that they've had in a lot of big corporations is they try to use Arthur Andersen to solve problems. It's not Arthur Andersen who needs to solve the problems. It's the founder, it's the president, it's the VP of marketing who'd better be able to sit down at their computer and in a dialogue of six e-mails back and forth get someone to say, "Yes, I'll buy your product" or "Yes, send a salesperson." But they don't want to do that. They try to delegate it and when they do, they end up behind.

Colombo: So, does it all come down to clear thinking about the nature of the relationship between the company and the customer and constantly thinking about what the company can bring to the table?

Godin: It's very simple. It's about making promises and keeping them. You make a promise: "If you do this, I will do that." And then you do everything you can to keep the promise. And *only* that promise, not "Click here and we will review your last year's tax return absolutely free" and then take their e-mail address and data and start selling them 500 other things. You didn't promise to do that, so don't do it.

Colombo: The idea of permission, to be able to implement escalating permission effectively over time, though, is kind of like opening the kimono or doing a dance to move further down the aisle.

Godin: That's it. It's a series of incremental promises.

Colombo: In terms of creating value that makes sense from the customer's standpoint, is that something that by its nature is distinct and unique for each company?

Godin: There is no magic, you-must-do-it-this-way, you-must-do-it-that-way formula. There's a bunch of rules of thumb that we know and that you can learn over time, but it's very different for your doctor than it is for the guy who mows your lawn.

Colombo: And is it fair to say that anticipated communications are more effective if they're done in a way that is regular and periodic as opposed to sporadic?

Godin: It's certainly more anticipated if it's regular. Regular doesn't have to mean every week. It could mean every time the Olympics are running. But it can't be anticipated if it's random.

Colombo: What's the key point that small-business people should remember about permission-based marketing?

Godin: Small-business people spend most of their time reacting and almost none of their time *proactively* plotting their course, because there are just so many things for them to do. But permission marketing is extraordinarily urgent. It's not some new Internet gimmick. This is what marketing is going to be about for the foreseeable future. And because of that, you have to decide if you want to fight a holding action and stay the way you were or use this as an opportunity to dramatically and fundamentally change your business. The example I love to use is my dad, who's the world's largest manufacturer of hospital cribs—and hospital cribs never wear out, so it's hard to stay at that position. So he has totally changed the organization of his company to be permission-focused. As a result he's cut his marketing expenses by 30 or 40 percent and increased his sales by 30 or 40 percent. You don't have to do much math to figure out that that's a really good thing.

Colombo: Absolutely. Would it be accurate to say that in today's business environment, a holding position is not an option anymore?

Godin: I was just thinking of the *Thomas Register*. I'm trying to buy some wire baskets for my office, and two thirds of the companies listed don't have a Web site. So, it's possible for some companies to try to ignore the whole thing. It's possible to say, "We have 15 clients, all of whom wear short-sleeved shirts with pocket protectors, and we're just going to deal with them and that's that." And that's okay; that's a holding action and it might last until you retire. I mean, you could milk it for maybe another few years. Just make sure that you're not planning on waiting too long before you retire!

Chapter 14

Online Odds and Ends

This chapter is a kind of catchall, comprised of some important matters that didn't quite fit in anywhere else in this book. The first couple deal with aspects of extending your business out to the Internet that you might not have thought much about before. These are "here and now" considerations that will make the Web component of your business more effective and more customer-friendly. These last few items will offer you some glimpses into the future that will help you keep your online sales and marketing activities on track even while the technological environment in which you do business keeps changing at breakneck speed.

24×7 (Twenty-four by Seven)

It used to be almost impossible to find a "real world" business that was open 24 hours a day, 7 days a week. (L.L. Bean in Freeport, Maine was one well-known exception. Steak N Shake, to the delight of several generations of teenagers, was another.) Recently, more businesses—most notably pharmacies and supermarkets—have adopted this model, but it is still very much the exception rather than the rule. On the Web, though, it's important to remember that you're open for business all the time. Depending on what you're trying to do with your Web site, it may not have much of a practical impact. On the other hand, there may be representations you make on your site that are based on unconscious assumptions about when people are visiting. For example, you might invite a prospect to fill in a form and promise a certain response time. You'll want to make sure that response time allows for the fact that your customer may be surfing the Web at three in the morning!

This aspect of the Web also underscores the significance of the Circuit City strategy that I described in Chapter 6. In fact, it can be a key to your strategy of linking your Web site to your "real world" operations. For example, what if you gave your customers the ability to order something from you on the Web just before they turned in at night and then pick it up from one of your stores when they're on the way in to work in the morning? You'd probably have to adjust your in-store operations to accommodate an influx of early customers, but the competitive advantage would be considerable.

Globalization

This is one of those artful terms of "consultant-speak" that you might have come across on CNBC or in a business magazine and dismissed as not being relevant to your business. Expanding your business on to the Web might force you to think again.

A couple of years ago, a woman I know in a small town in Pennsylvania operated a modest retail store from which she sold wonderful, unique pieces of hand-crafted jewelry. Mediocre sales and relatively high overhead motivated her to move her business to the Web, where she thought she'd be able to extend her reach beyond the confines of her local market. Her very first customer on the Web turned out to be in Zimbabwe. Talk about using the Web to extend your reach!

Here's the point: If you structure your business so that you're actually conducting transactions from your Web site, it's likely that you're going to wind up addressing issues that you never had to consider before.

The first issue is whether you are, in fact, willing to fulfill orders from outside the U.S. If so, are there any limits on where you're willing to sell? Canada? Mexico? Beyond those?

If you think you want to do business outside of the U.S., you've got to consider how you're going to get paid. Are you able to accept payment in foreign currencies? You'll also want to think about international shipping and customs issues. Obviously, these are all wrinkles that are not present when the boundaries of your market are defined by a store or sales office.

None of these issues is insurmountable. You may very well transform yourself into a "global" enterprise quite readily. What I'm suggesting, though, is that these are some issues that you might want to think about before that first order arrives from halfway around the world!

The Changing Communications Infrastructure

The first modem I ever bought hummed along at 300 baud. Compared to today's communications options, it seems quaint and archaic. It wasn't too long ago that my old Hayes modem was considered a state-of-the-art speed demon. And it won't be too long from now that the 56K modems your customers are using to dial up and log on to the Internet will seem just as quaint and archaic as my Hayes modem seems today.

This is not merely interesting speculation. If the Internet is an integral part of your business model, then it's important that you think about the nature of the changes that the future is sure to bring. If you owned a store downtown, you'd want to know what sorts of zoning changes the city council has in mind for your block, wouldn't you? This is really the same kind of issue. Here, then, are some of the issues that you'll want to take into consideration as you position yourself not just for today's wired world but for the wired world that is certainly on its way tomorrow:

Broadband (Part 1): Speed

Some time in the not-too-distant future, dialing up to access the Internet will be about as common as booting your computer up from a floppy. Experts aren't sure when this is coming, but there's no doubt in anyone's mind that it's on the way.

One or more high-speed technologies will replace today's dial-up access. Cable modems and DSL are the two most prevalent options today. Whether it is one of these or a combination of the two or, perhaps, something else entirely that finally displaces dial-up access doesn't matter for the purposes of our discussion. What does matter is how the speed of the new technology is going to impact what you do on the Web. Here are some of the questions you might want to ask yourself:

@   What would I add to my Web site if speed was not an issue?

@   How could I use real time audio?

@   How could I use real time video?

@   How would my customers behave differently if they could access my site with a *much* faster connection?

@ If speed on the Web was no longer an issue, how could that affect my store or sales office?

@ Is there someplace in my business model I could be blindsided by a competitor who's "built for speed"?

@ Is there any way that I could blindside a competitor if I were "built for speed"?

Significant improvements in speed change more than the rate at which things can happen. They change the nature of the way in which people use things. When you can fly across the country in four and a half hours instead of driving across country in four or five days, the significance is not just that you get there faster. The significance is that you'll undertake the four and a half hour trip for reasons that would never justify the four day trip. The change in speed changes the nature of what a cross country trip means and how it's used. The same principle applies when it comes to speed on the Web. Broadband means more than just working faster.

There's no question about the fact that high-speed Internet access is well on its way to becoming ubiquitous. The only question is: When it does, will your business be ready for it?

Bandwidth (Part 2): Constant Connections

When broadband connections become the norm rather than the exception, higher connection speeds are an obvious difference from the standard dial-up connections that most of your customers are using today. But broadband connections will be different in another way that is a little more subtle, maybe, but no less important. Unlike dial-up connections, your customers' broadband connections to the Internet will always be on.

That doesn't seem as though it's a big difference, but it will change the landscape with regard to the kinds of services that your customers will find practical to use on the Internet. Let me give you a couple of examples.

Today, for the most part, your customers are not using the Internet to look up phone numbers. It's too much of a bother to dial up to get the number of, say, the local pizza joint. If there's a persistent Internet connection, though, it's very likely that behavior will change because the time advantage switches from the phone book to the Web. (With persistent Internet connections, people tend to leave their computers on all the time, so booting up will not be a factor in the equation.) If you have a business that has a local geography as its market, this small change in consumer behavior will have big implications for you.

Another example would be a Web site such as *Dictionary.com,* for all the same reasons. Today, the probability of a student using the Web as her primary resource to check a word's meaning is slight. If her computer had a persistent, high-speed Internet connection, though, it would be easier and faster than looking the word up in a regular dictionary.

Again, now is a good time to be asking yourself some questions that will help you position your business for the future:

@   What services would my customers want from me (that they don't necessarily want today) if I could provide them online and instantly?

@   What information would my customers want from me (that they don't necessarily want today) if I could provide it online and instantly?

@   What kinds of things could I do if my customers had an always-on connection to my business?

Persistence, along with the enhanced speed of broadband connections, will cause significant changes in the ways that your customers use the Internet to connect and communicate with your business. Some of these changes will be obvious and predictable. Some of them, though, will catch all the experts and pundits by surprise. But if you're thinking about these issues creatively right now, they won't necessarily catch you by surprise. In fact, one of the great things about doing business in an environment of technological upheaval is the fact that your speculation can be as good as anyone else's about how the Internet is going to affect your business and your customers.

The Experts Speak

If you're like most businesspeople, technology is not your first concern. It's a tool to get a job done and, from a sales and marketing standpoint, you've always believed that job is taking care of your customer. But it's hard to open up a business book or magazine lately without being told by one expert after another that some aspect of technology—most often the Internet—is going to make everything you're doing obsolete or ineffective. You're being told that your way of doing business is yesterday's news. (Interestingly, the people who are telling you this have, for the most part, never actually run a business themselves, but are sure getting a lot of attention in the press.)

The message I want to leave you with is to trust *your* judgment—not the judgment of the so-called "experts"—when it comes to your business, your marketplace, and your customers. Don't count on the "experts" to tell you where your business needs to be because *they don't know.* The writers in the press don't know where all of this technological change is going to wind up. The endless parade of consultants and gurus who are quoted in the books and business magazines don't know. Even Bill Gates doesn't know for sure. (I'll grant you, though, that *his* guess is better than most!) The recent history of the high-tech industry offers ample evidence that users will make up their own minds about what is valuable and what is not. And, over the years, they've demonstrated a stubborn inclination to think for themselves and ignore the exhortations of the "experts."

From your perspective as a businessperson, as someone who is trying to increase the effectiveness of your sales and marketing efforts, it really doesn't matter to you today where all the technology is going to wind up in the long run. That's because, ultimately, it's not technology that's going to determine your sales and marketing success. It's your own unique ability to understand and then address the needs of your customers.

Let me give you an idea of what passes for strategic business thinking in the dotcom world. (Feel free to reflect on this the next time you feel intimidated by one of the "experts.") Here is a dotcom guru, quoted in a recent issue of *Wired*, explaining how a textbook publishing house ought to discard its suddenly outmoded business model in favor of a technology-based program:

> *You know what? You need to scrap all that other stuff, give away Palm VIIs to every student in the country, let them download books from your new information server. Now, the $30 they were paying Barnes & Noble, [the publisher] makes $3 on. Instead, just charge them $3.50. You're making more profit on your digital download than you did through your old value chain, but your new value chain says that you're giving away something free in exchange for multiple uses of something that doesn't cost you anything to distribute.*

Huh? Just *give away* a Palm VII (which, as of this writing, sells for $449)? So, all you've got to do is immediately and radically change the buying behavior of your customers, then sell 128 textbooks to each customer *before* you break even on the deal. On that 129th book, you can start rolling in dough. *That* is what passes for strategic business thinking among the "experts."

I know that you can do better than that. That's why I want to leave you with this message: In the grand scheme of things, the technology piece of the puzzle is relatively easy. There is plenty of talent out there that is available to help you get where you want to go. The hard part is knowing where to go. The hard part is understanding what your market wants. The hard part is understanding what motivates your customers. Servicing the needs and desires of your customers is the objective. Implementing technology is the vehicle that can get you there.

Am I saying that technology is unimportant? Of course not. Technology is a great enabler. It allows you to restructure your business, to make connections that were never before possible. The Internet represents a tremendous opportunity to redesign the ways in which you offer value to your marketplace.

What I am saying, though, is that technology is a tool which can only be used effectively by someone like you who understands marketing and selling. It can only be used effectively by someone like you who knows what the real objective is.

And in your business—in all of your sales and marketing efforts—the real objective is capturing customers.

Index

About the Author

Since the 1993 publication of his best-selling book, *Sales Force Automation,* George Colombo has been one of the country's most sought-after speakers on the subject of technology-enabled sales and marketing. In addition to a busy speaking schedule, George does extensive television and audio work for a blue-chip client list that includes IBM, several major software companies, and a number of trade associations.

A prolific writer and a dynamic presenter, George was recently named one of the ten most influential people in the history of the Customer Relationship Management industry by the industry's leading trade publication. His company, Influence Technologies, Inc., is based in Winter Springs, Florida. George can be reached via e-mail at *george@capturing customers.com.*